The Jumbo Sticker Fun Book

HERMES HOUSE

contents

Words

Count the cans
of food.

Do you like balloons
that go bang?

Find a trumpet for the
animal musicians.

How many flowers
can you see?

Where are the fish?

Do you play music on a
cassette tape player?

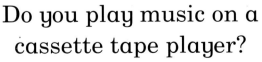

Music

recorder

cassette tape player

cymbals

drum

Find another cassette tape to play

tambourine

trumpet

saxophone

Can you find the cymbals for the teddy bear to play?

xylophone

musical notes

I want to play the drum too! Can you find one for me?

Find another teddy bear to join the band.

6

Birthday

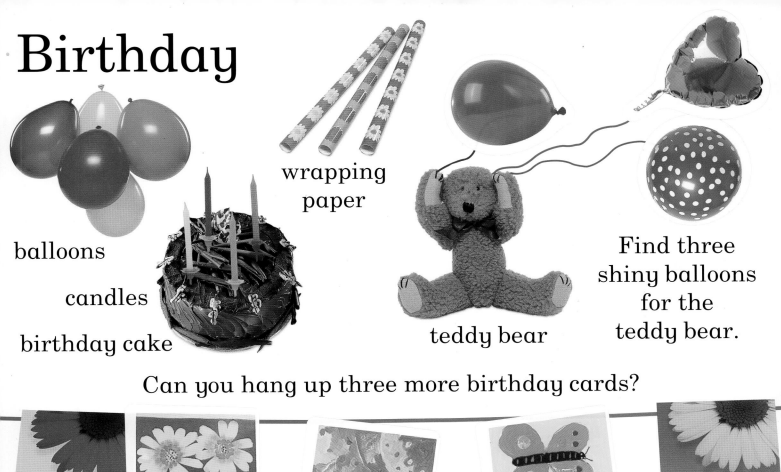

balloons

candles

birthday cake

wrapping paper

teddy bear

Find three shiny balloons for the teddy bear.

Can you hang up three more birthday cards?

Stick more shiny bows on the birthday presents.

party streamers

juice

straw

soda pop

plastic cups

presents

party hat

I wonder what's inside!

Find the puppy with the extra birthday card.

Toys and games

teddy bear

spinning tops

doll

Can you find two more spinning tops?

tricycle

puzzle

dice

Can you find Lucy another rope to skip with?

rocking horse

Find a teddy bear to ride on the rocking horse.

marbles

ball

Can you build more blocks to make a very tall tower?

springy toy

8

Shapes

stars

Can you find two more stars?

triangle

spiral

square

wiggly lines

heart

circle

Find some rings and fit them inside this hoop.

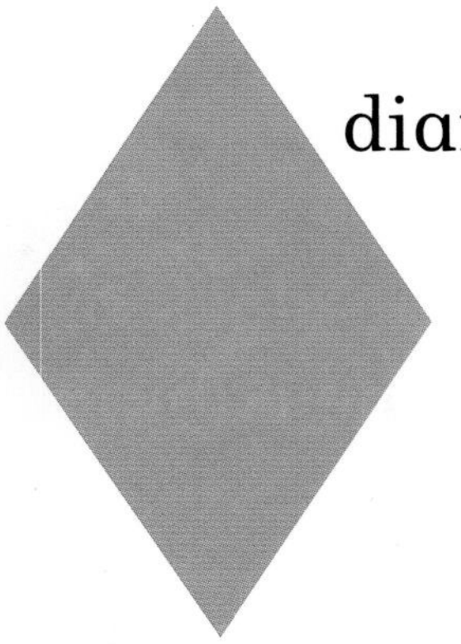

diamond

flowers

semicircle

9

At home

lamp

books

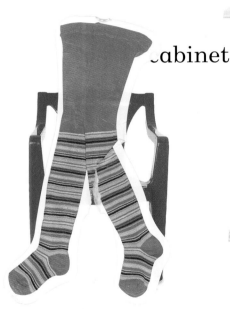

cabinet

Put the teapot on the table.

Put the clock on top of the cabinet.

telephone

10

Can you match the sticker words and pictures?

plant pot

Bathtime

Can you find three more fun soaps?

toothbrush

Find Alice some bathtime friends.

Find another red bath sponge.

sponge

bath whale

Find more whales and ducks to float on the water.

towel

bath ducks

toilet paper

Stick the right words next to the bathtime pictures.

11

Clothes

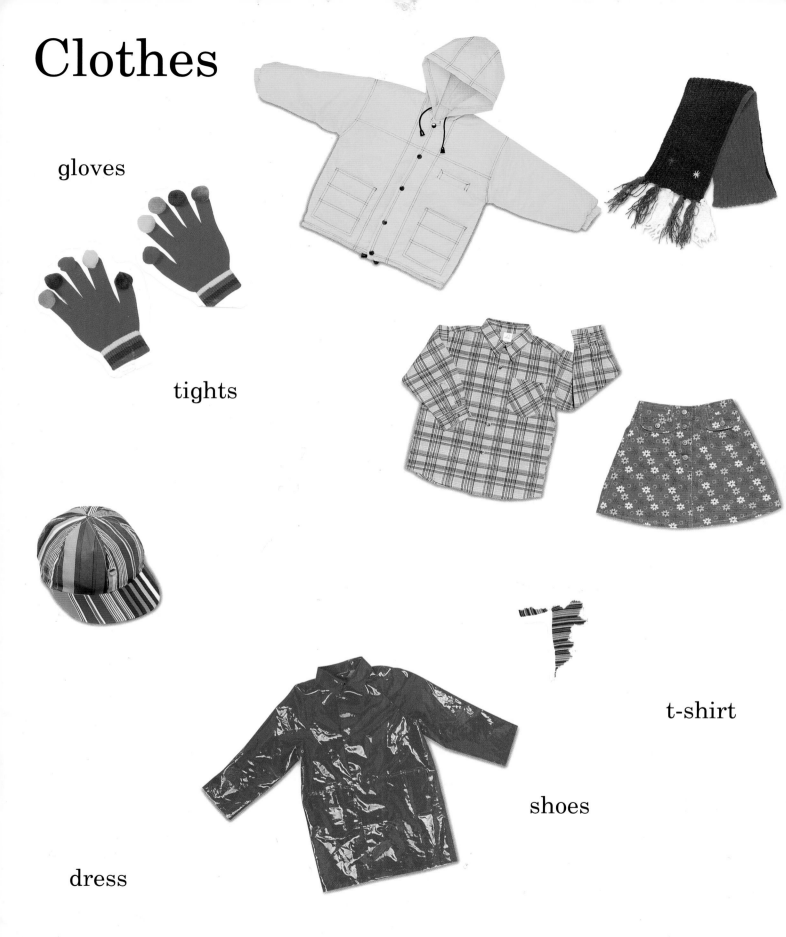

gloves

tights

dress

t-shirt

shoes

Can you match the stickers
to the words and pictures?

12

Transport

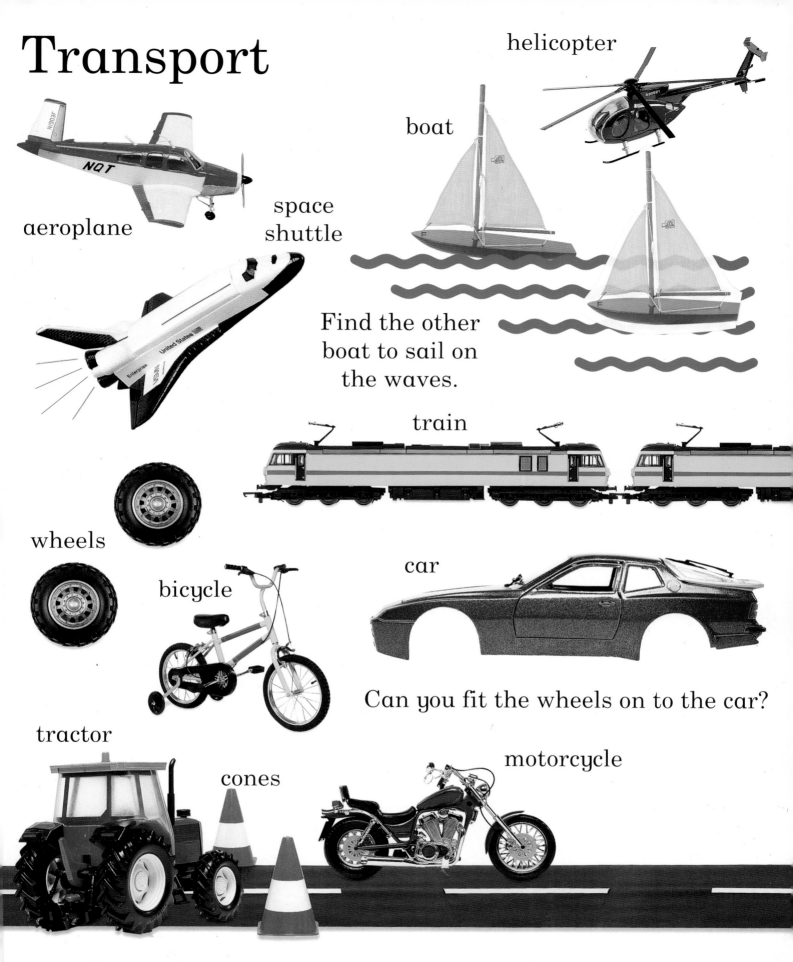

helicopter

boat

aeroplane

space shuttle

Find the other boat to sail on the waves.

train

wheels

bicycle

car

Can you fit the wheels on to the car?

tractor

cones

motorcycle

Direct the traffic by adding new cones to the road.

Bugs

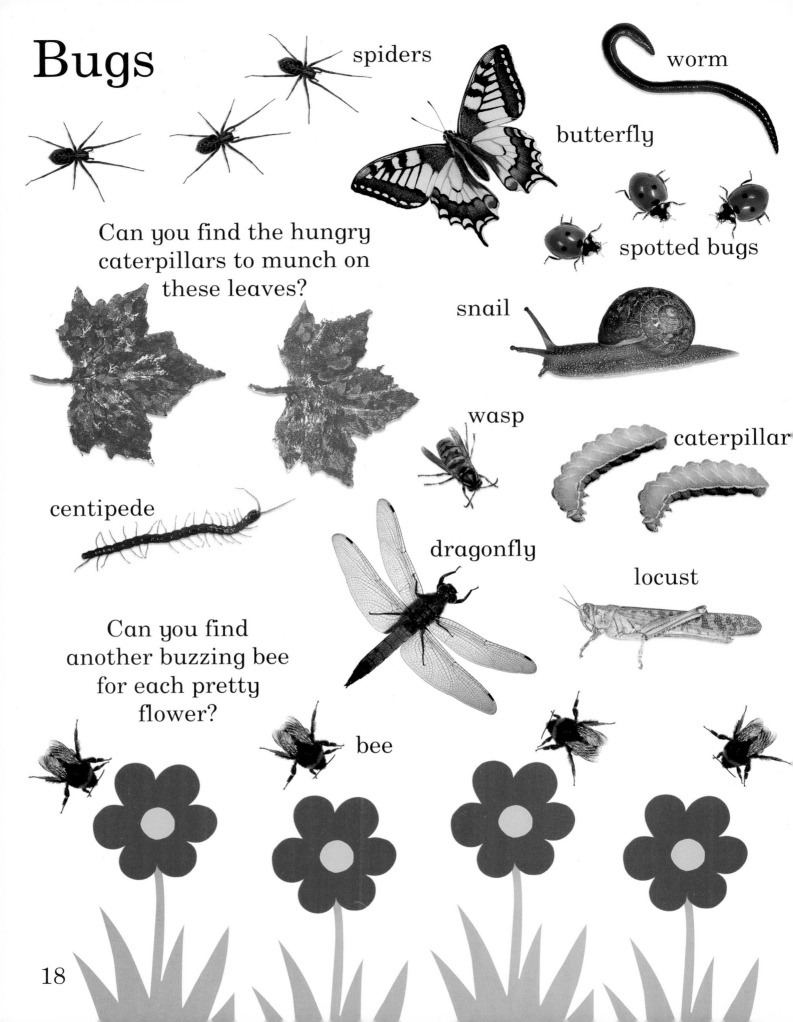

spiders

worm

butterfly

spotted bugs

Can you find the hungry caterpillars to munch on these leaves?

snail

wasp

caterpillar

centipede

dragonfly

locust

Can you find another buzzing bee for each pretty flower?

bee

18

Animals

Who is the fastest animal in the race?

sheep

horse

chicken

rabbits

tortoises

fish

Can you find a swimming partner for this fish?

Find some baby chicks.

Find two more leaping frogs.

hamster

piglet

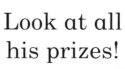

Look at all his prizes!

The puppy wins the race!

cat

mouse

This cat wants to eat. Can you find his bowl?

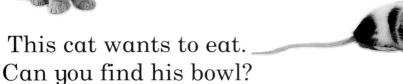

19

My Body and Me

How many children are sitting cross-legged?

Sitting down uses muscles.

Can you see David's lungs?

I like playing sport.

Have you heard your heartbeat?

Watch Amy do a backbend.

You and your body

Each part of you has a different name.

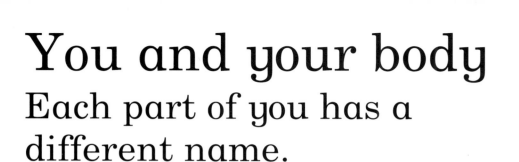

Fred the skeleton stretches out his arms and legs.

Anna can stretch too... can you?

feet

hand

Philip stands with feet apart and arms out wide.

Lisa touches her elbow.

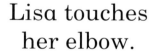

Can you find the boy touching his ear and nose?

Can you match the labels to the body parts?

Can you find the safety helmet to protect Anna's head?

Where is my sparkling tiara?

I wear pretty beads in my hair.

Hair grows on your head...

...I have long hair.

23

Lungs
We breathe in air to give us life.

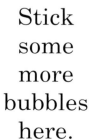

lungs

We use our lungs to breathe in and out...

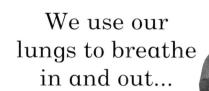

...you can see the air filling up the bag.

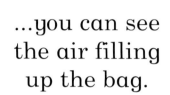

Can you find the lungs sticker?

Anna is making bubbles by blowing air out of her lungs.

Stick some more bubbles here.

Take a deep breath, then blow!

Heart

Our hearts never stop beating while we are alive.

This is what your heart looks like.

Can you find the sticker heart shape?

Look! Andrew is listening to his brother's heartbeat.

Billy is taking his pulse to see how fast his heart is beating.

Can you feel your pulse?

25

Muscles

We use our muscles all the time.

Look! Amy can use her muscles to arch her back.

Paula uses leg muscles to hop around.

Bouncing uses lots of muscles.

Are these children pushing or pulling?

Muscles help us to push and pull.

26

I'm stretching my arm muscles.

You need strong muscles to climb a rope.

You even use muscles to sit down.

Chewing uses muscles too.

Can you find some food for lunch?

Could you lift a heavy wheelbarrow?

Find more teddy bears to make the wheelbarrow heavier.

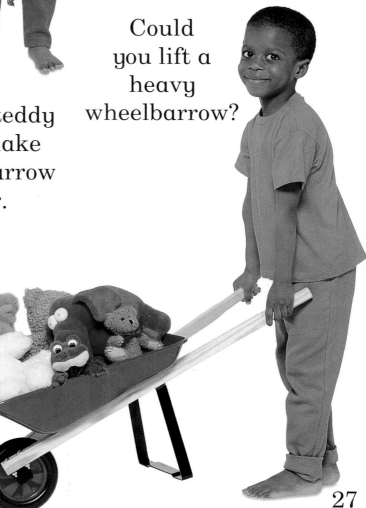

27

Skin and bone

We are all made of skin and bone.

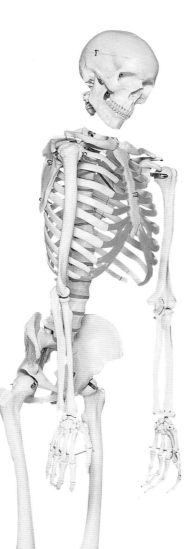

Can you find Fred's sticker skull?

Our bones are covered by our skin.

Our knees are bones called joints and so are our elbows.

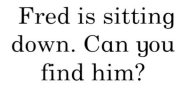

All our bones make a skeleton.

Fred is sitting down. Can you find him?

We have bones which means we are not floppy like jellyfish.

When we are cold our skin gets goosebumps.

Sarah is lying down.

So is Fred!

Can you find another feather duster to tickle the foot with?

Exercising makes our skin sweat.

Can you find the teddy bear badminton partner?

Skin covers our bodies.

It is soft and supple, and stretches too!

Senses

These enable us to see, hear, feel, taste and smell.

Glasses can help us to see clearly.

We hear with our ears.

Stick on some more loud musical notes.

What are the children listening to?

We see with our

Ouch! This feels sharp and prickly.

You your to re this!

We smell with our noses.

Phew – smelly shoes!

Laura's sweater feels soft and smells fresh.

Find something that looks pretty and smells nice.

Can you find stickers of something that feels furry, something that tastes sweet and something that tastes sour?

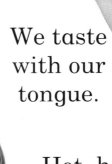

We taste with our tongue.

We touch with our skin.

Pop! This feels funny!

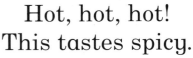

Hot, hot, hot! This tastes spicy.

31

Growing Up
Our bodies grow all the time.

small
girl

teenager

bigger girl

tiny baby

Can you find the baby more toys to play with?

Can you find the labels to match their heights?

Does this outfit still fit?

Find Peter some clothes that will fit him.

Sarah wants to grow quickly.

Now she wants to grow slowly.

To grow strong we must keep fit!

Am I growing now?

33

My healthy body

We must eat fresh fruit.

Can you find some more healthy fruit?

Can you find two furry friends to sleep on the end of Lisa's bed?

Honey popcorn tastes good but it may harm your teeth...

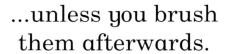

Lisa is keeping fit by exercising.

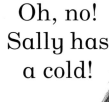

...unless you brush them afterwards.

Oh, no! Sally has a cold!

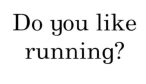

Do you like running?

Can you find her some medicine?

34

Funny faces
Each expression we make shows how we are feeling.

a happy face

Can you roll your tongue?

a fish face

Can you find another fish face?

I'm puzzled.

a cheeky face

35

Make and build

Sam makes pancakes for breakfast.

Two clever children make pretty pictures.

Find some paints, scissors and glue that the children can make pictures with.

What is Thomas making?

Matthew is building a tower.

Look at the tall tower that Rebecca has built!

Which is the tallest tower?

Finish building the tower of toys.

Dragon builds a tower with toy bricks.

37

At play

Julie
plays the
trumpet loudly!

Do you play
badminton?

Use the stickers to
play this game.

one, two, three, four, five ...

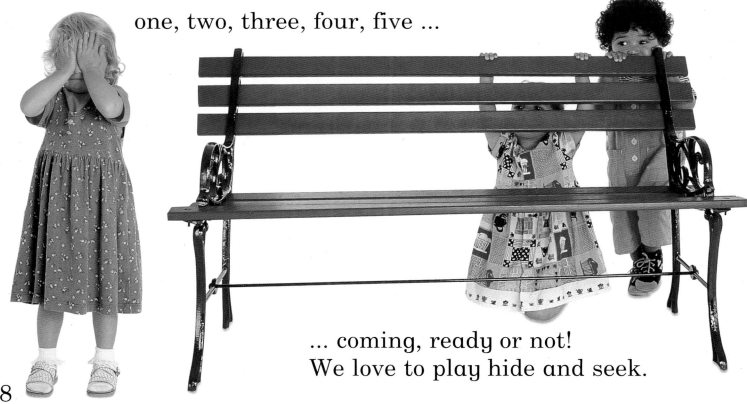

... coming, ready or not!
We love to play hide and seek.

I like hopping for fun.

Susie loves to skip.

Lisa likes to jump...

...but Mark can jump higher!

Find the objects the children are jumping over.

39

Water fun

We splash in the pool.

I wash the dishes.

Let's pour water over our mother!

Find the fishes to swim in the sea.

40

Look and see

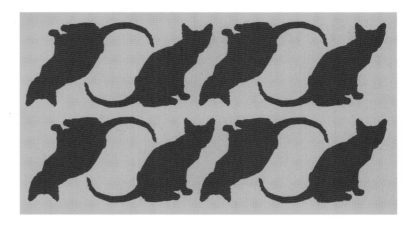

See how many
carrots there are.

Look for the cats in this
picture. How many can you see?

Find the insects
that Sara is
looking at.

Can you see the 10
differences between
these pictures?

Growing

A flower bud opens into a beautiful flower.

Little children grow into adults.

Find small clothes for the child and large clothes for the adult.

Nails grow long, if you don't cut them.

Tiny puppies grow bigger...

and bigger...

and bigger still.

Going to work

A detective hunts for clues.

A chef cooks meals.

A carpenter uses tools.

A doctor heals patients.

Put the carpenter's tools on the shelf.

Dressing up

I'm getting dressed.

I am wearing summer clothes.

I like to wrap up warmly on a cold day.

I am wearing my nightclothes for bed.

Stick more summer clothes here.

Stick more winter clothes here.

44

Lunch time

Let's enjoy the tasty party food.

Peter is nibbling these yummy cookies.

Put more party treats here.

Lucy and Simon are eating lunch.

45

Shopping

I push my groceries through the supermarket.

Harriet writes her shopping list.

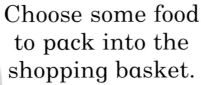

Choose some food to pack into the shopping basket.

Laura serves at the till.

46

Tidying up

Peter cleans his room.

Ben irons his clothes.

I am mopping the floor.

Find the cleaning things to put into the bowl.

What am I doing?

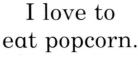

I love to
eat popcorn.

I clean my
bowl after
eating
breakfast.

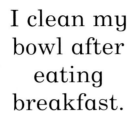

Find some more
clean plates.

I can hop
around on
one leg.

It is great
fun to jump
in the air.

48

Do you like to build sandcastles on the beach?

Stick more sandcastles here.

I can play a song on my guitar.

Liam carries the shopping basket home.

Karen draws a picture.

49

Making Groups

Can you find
three balls?

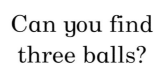

Where is the pair
of gloves?

Can you see four
toy dumpers?

Where are the triangle
shaped presents?

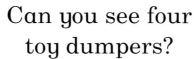

Four children are
having fun.

Can you find a pair
of footprints?

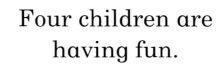

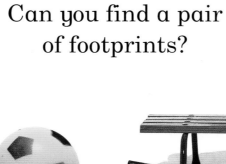

Sorting by color

You can make groups of things that are the same color.

red

strawberries

tomato

Find another red fruit.

gloves

green

grapes

iguana

Stick a green fruit here.

food monster

blue

toy whale

snakes

pants

Find more blue bowling pins.

yellow

maracas

flower

Find another yellow flower.

bananas

52

Two by two
A pair is two identical things.

a pair of socks

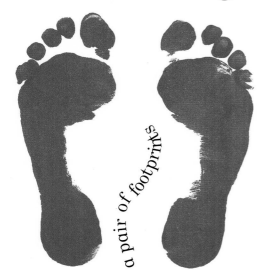

a pair of footprints

a pair of gloves

Find what is missing here.

Partners go together.

knife and fork

witch and cauldron

Find the sticker to go with the racket.

Shapes

Groups can be made with things that are the same shape.

squares

picture frame

stamp

Miss Smith
84 Woodlane
Avenue
Anytown, USA
12345

envelope

candy

Find the square.

triangles ▲

present

slices of cake

Find the present that fits this space.

hat

rectangles

Which present matches this shape?

xylophone

ruler

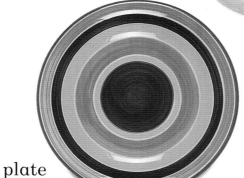
present

circles ●
clock

plate

steering wheel

Find the circular cookies to put on the plate.

54

Matching patterns

You can group by matching patterns together.

stripes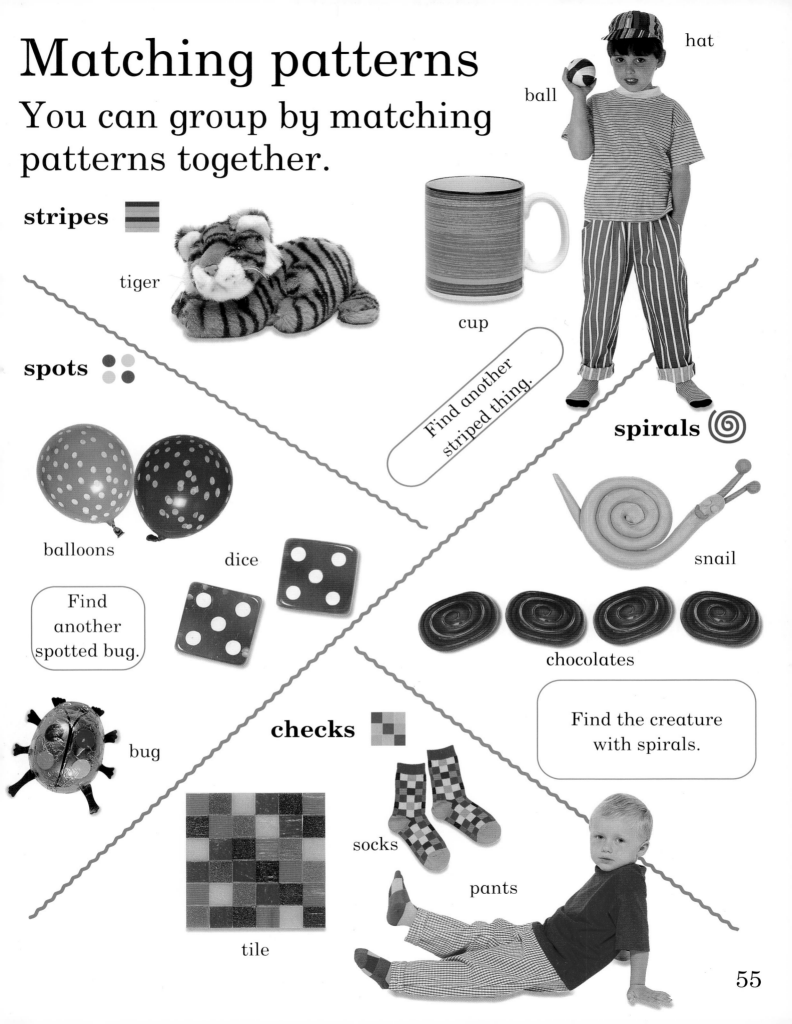

tiger

cup

hat

ball

Find another striped thing.

spots

balloons

dice

Find another spotted bug.

bug

spirals

snail

chocolates

Find the creature with spirals.

checks

socks

tile

pants

55

Grouping by size

You can sort big and small things.

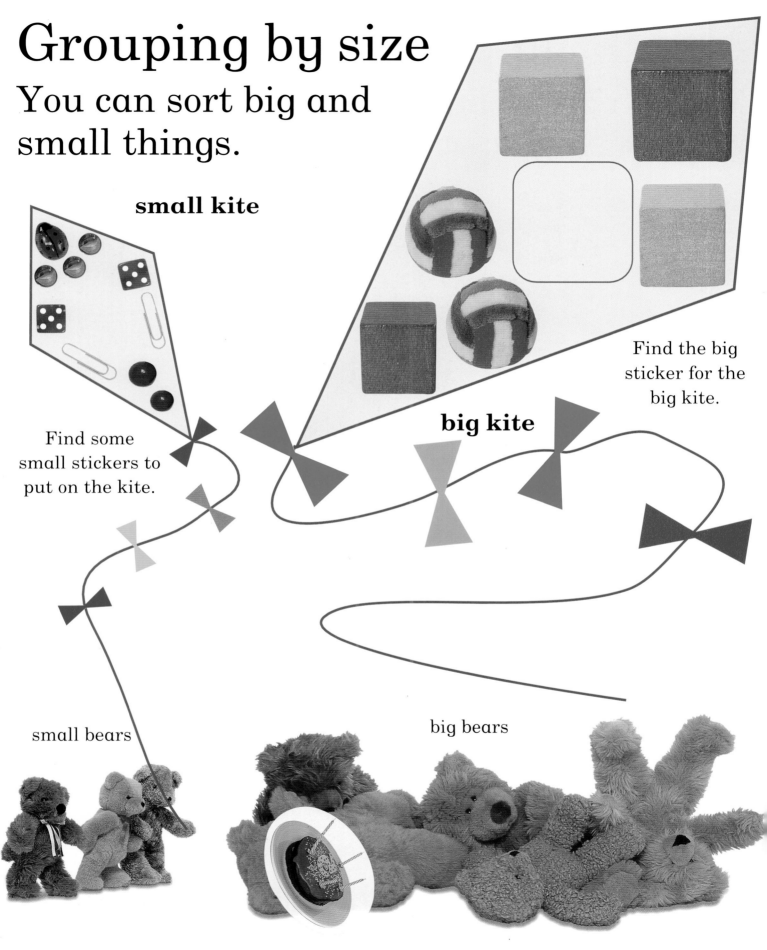

small kite

big kite

Find some small stickers to put on the kite.

Find the big sticker for the big kite.

small bears

big bears

Animal groups
You can sort animals by where they live.

farm animals

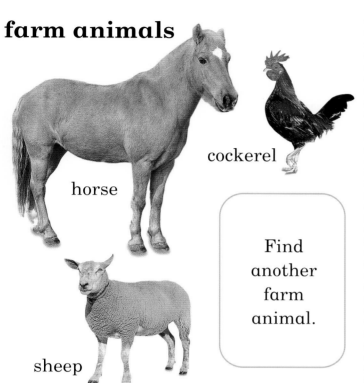

cockerel

horse

Find another farm animal.

sheep

pet animals

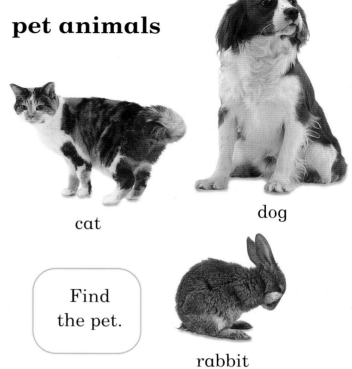

cat

dog

Find the pet.

rabbit

flying insects

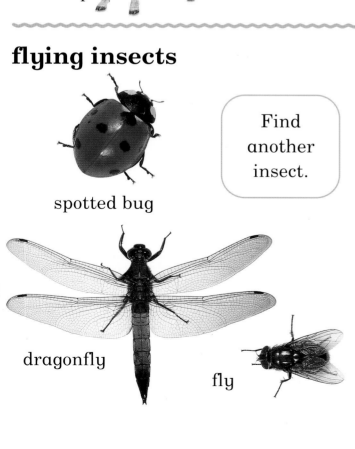

spotted bug

Find another insect.

dragonfly

fly

wild animals

Find another wild animal.

monkey

rhinoceros

crocodile

Summer and winter

Groups can be made from things that belong in summer and winter.

summer

Find the summer sticker.

wading pool

T-shirt

buckets

shovel

honeysuckle

ice cream

winter

snowman

ivy

snowflake

holly

Find some more snowflakes.

snow

sled

58

Types of clothes

Keep your clothes tidy by sorting them into groups.

On which part of the body are these worn?

...and these?

pants

skirt

bathing suit

shorts

jacket

shirts

What would you do in these?

What do people wear at night?

leotard

sneakers

baby sleepsuit

bathrobe

slippers

Food

Different types of food are grouped together in stores and in your home.

fruit

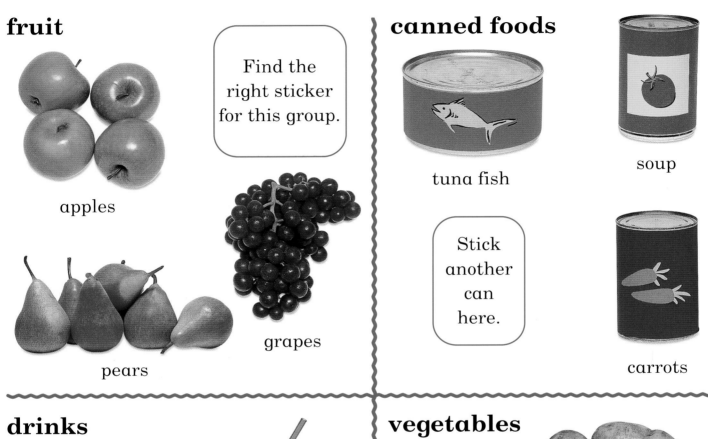

apples

Find the right sticker for this group.

pears

grapes

canned foods

tuna fish

soup

Stick another can here.

carrots

drinks

orange juice

milkshake

What can you stick here?

milk

vegetables

onions

potatoes

Which is the right sticker for this group?

cauliflowers

Toy store

Can you name all these different types of toys?

model toys

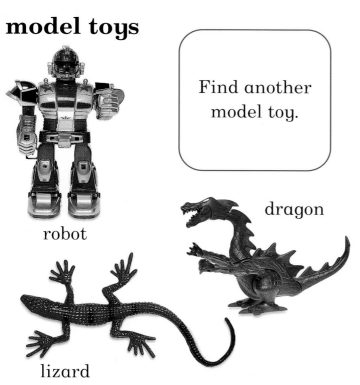

Find another model toy.

robot

dragon

lizard

trucks

bulldozer

tractor

Stick the right toy for this group here.

dump truck

balls

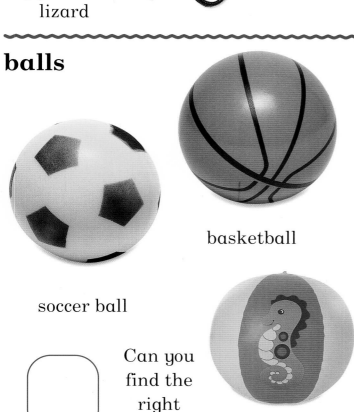

basketball

soccer ball

Can you find the right sticker?

beach ball

stuffed toys

Stick on another stuffed toy to join the group.

teddy bear

octopus

tiger

61

On the ground and in the air

These things move along
the ground on wheels.

motorcycle

Find the
tricycle.

toy electric train

Find
another
car.

Find the toy train.

bicycle

Find
some more
roller skates.

toy car

roller skates

skateboard

62

Aircraft fly high in the air.

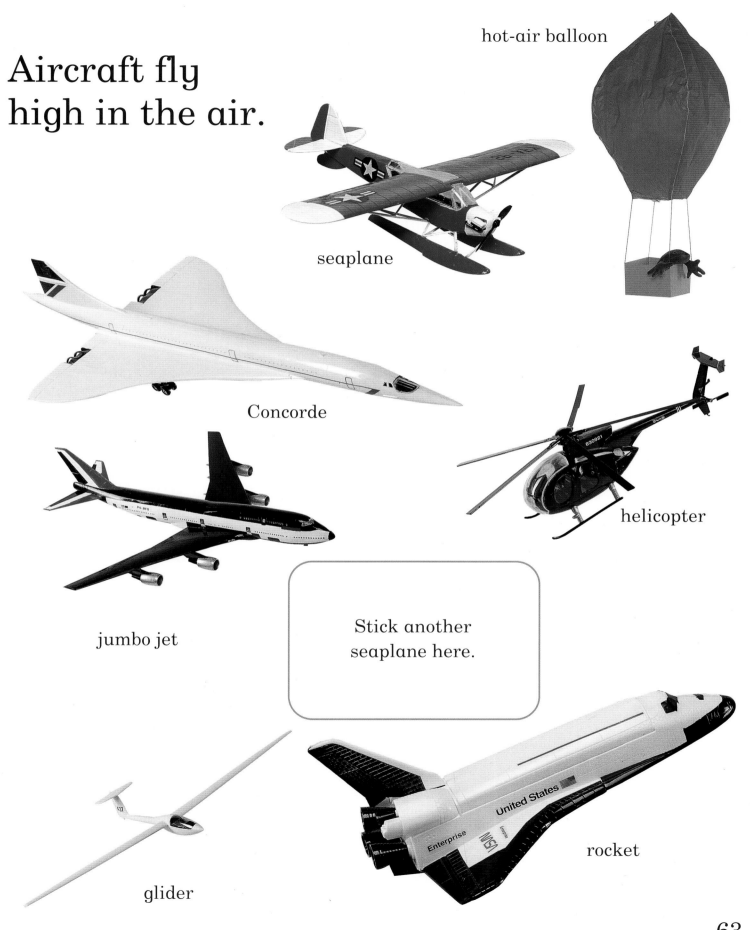

hot-air balloon

seaplane

Concorde

helicopter

jumbo jet

Stick another seaplane here.

glider

rocket

All kinds of groups

Find the names of each group and stick them in the right places.

What color?

Which pattern?

What shape?

Which season?

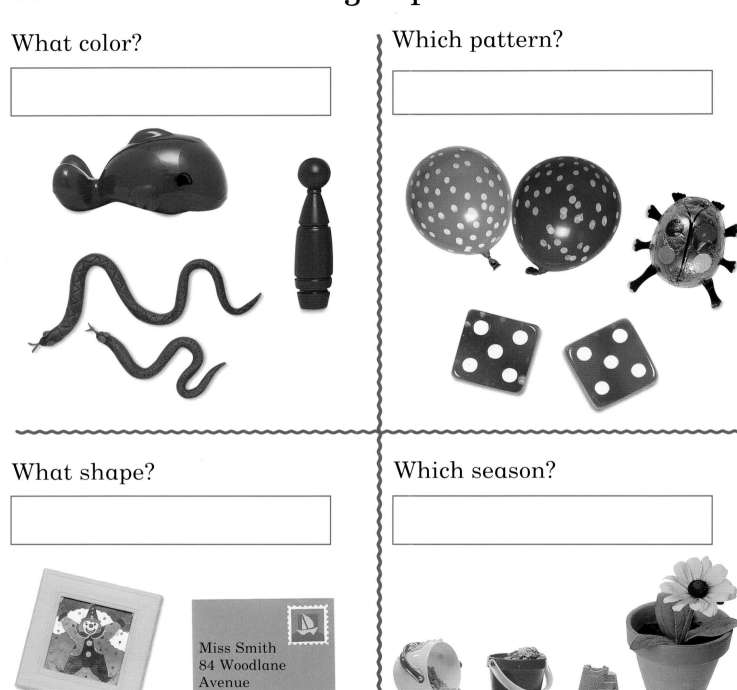

When do people wear these clothes?

What type of food?

What kind of toys?

Where would you find these?

Counting
and Sums

Can you count the
balancing bears?

How many legs does the
kitten have?

Can you count the
surprise presents?

How many slippery
snails are there?

How many potato heads
do you see?

How many fingers is
Jenny holding up?

Can you see two bottles
of juice?

0 to 5

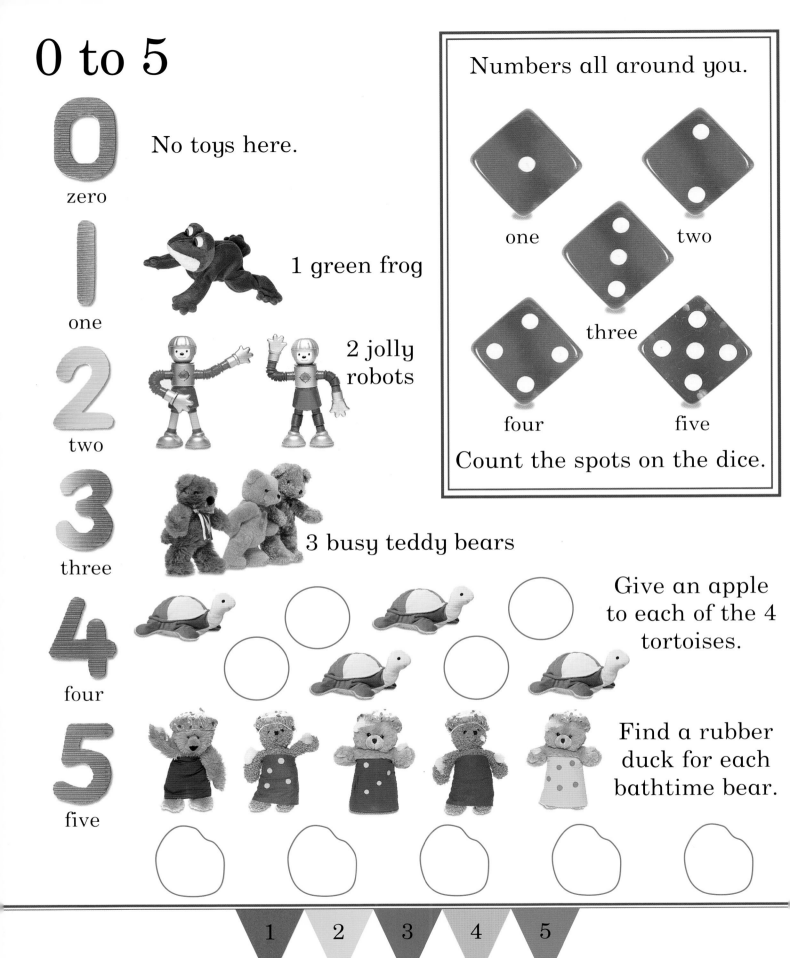

0 zero — No toys here.

1 one — 1 green frog

2 two — 2 jolly robots

3 three — 3 busy teddy bears

4 four — Give an apple to each of the 4 tortoises.

5 five — Find a rubber duck for each bathtime bear.

Numbers all around you.

one   two

three

four   five

Count the spots on the dice.

1 2 3 4 5

6 to 10

6
six

6 party animals

Numbers all around you.

Count the numbers on the clock.

7
seven

7 scary pirates

8
eight

8 blue aliens

9
nine

9 fire-breathing dragons

10
ten

| 1 | 2 | 3 | 4 | 5 |
| 6 | 7 | 8 | 9 | 10 |

Stick the 10 yellow octopuses here.

6 7 8 9 10

Up to twenty

Find the missing kittens
to count up to 20.

twenty

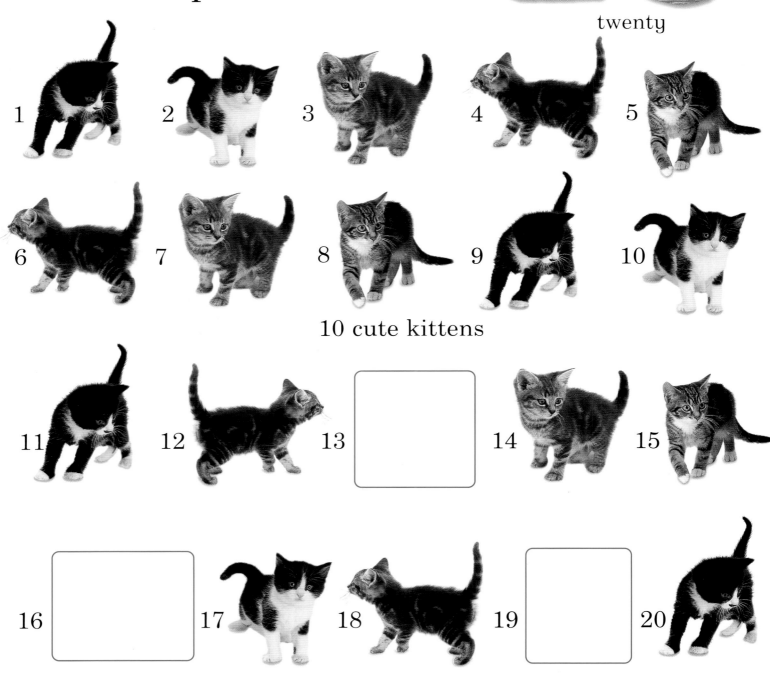

1

2

3

4

5

6

7

8

9

10

10 cute kittens

11

12

13

14

15

16

17

18

19

20

20 cute kittens altogether

Up to thirty

Count 3 groups of 10 to make 30 butterflies.

thirty

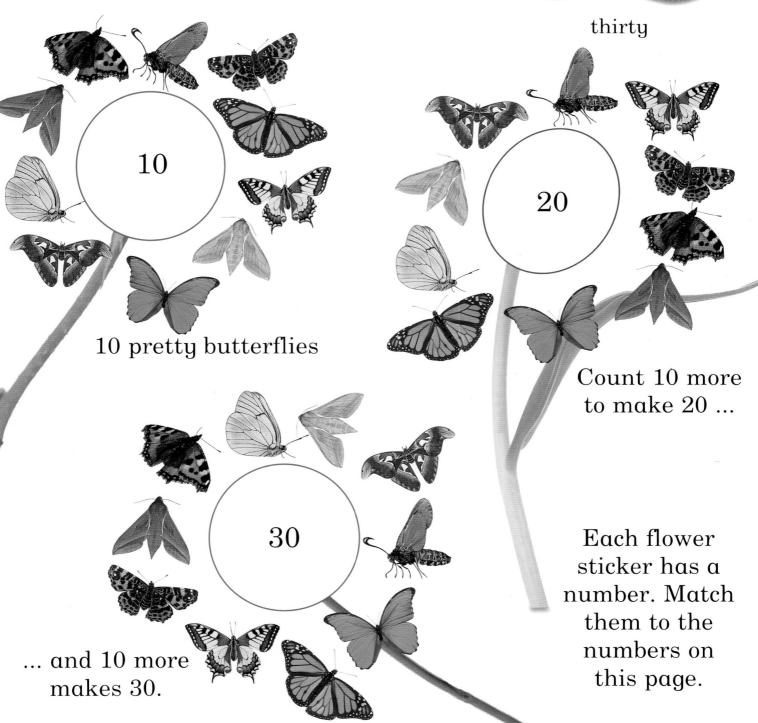

10

10 pretty butterflies

20

Count 10 more to make 20 ...

30

... and 10 more makes 30.

Each flower sticker has a number. Match them to the numbers on this page.

| 21 | 22 | 23 | 24 | 25 | 26 | 27 | 28 | 29 | 30 |

Up to forty

Find the missing musical instruments to make 40.

forty

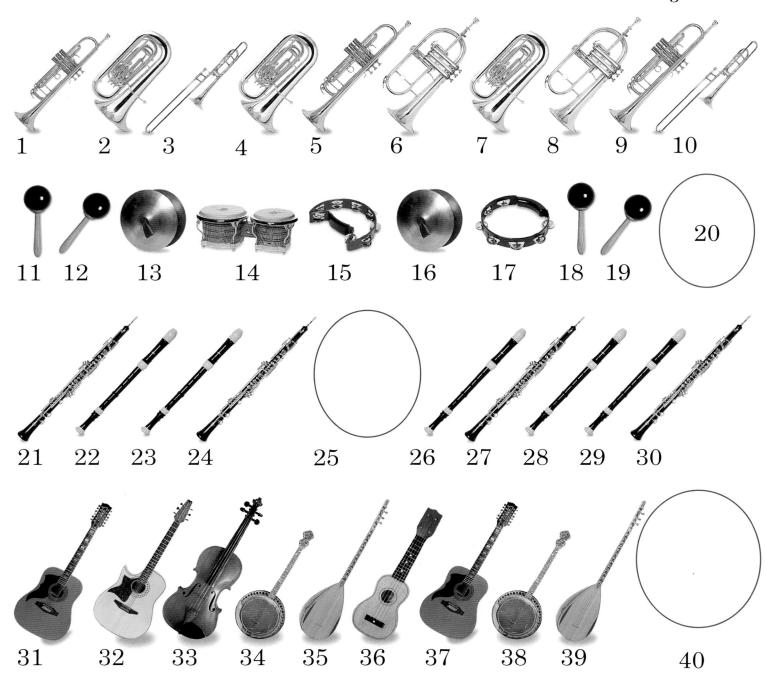

1   2   3   4   5   6   7   8   9   10

11   12   13   14   15   16   17   18   19   20

21   22   23   24   25   26   27   28   29   30

31   32   33   34   35   36   37   38   39   40

31   32   33   34   35   36   37   38   39   40

Up to fifty

How many things has Lisa put in each room to make 50?

fifty

the kitchen

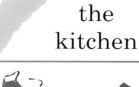

10

the living room

20

the garden

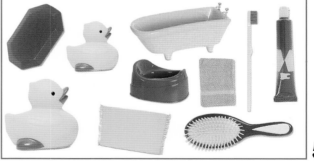

30

the bedroom

40

The missing flags are even numbers. They go up in twos. Put them in the right places.

the bathroom

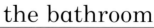

50

41   43   45   47   48   49

Up to sixty

There are 10 flowers in each bunch. Count 60 flowers.

sixty

Match the watering cans to the numbers.

10

20

30

40

50

60

Up to seventy

How many seaside things can you count?

seventy

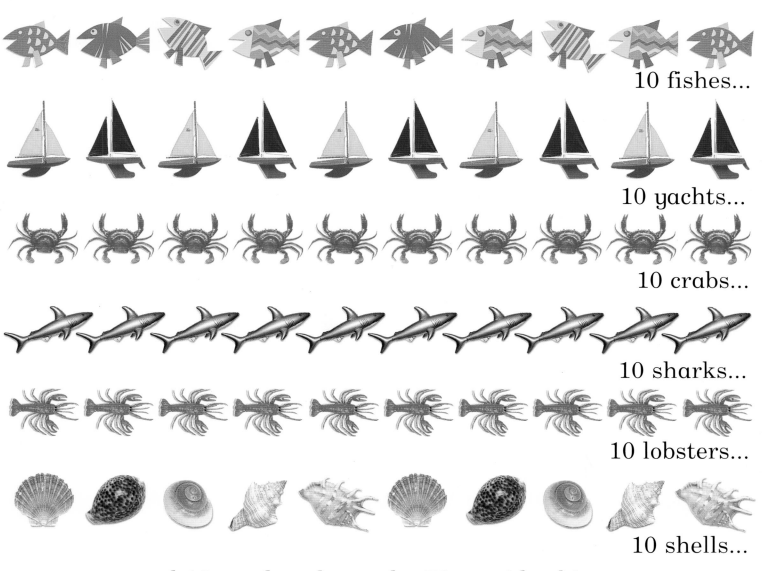

10 fishes...

10 yachts...

10 crabs...

10 sharks...

10 lobsters...

10 shells...

...and 10 sandcastles make 70 seaside objects.

Put the flags in the right order on the sandcastles.

| 61 | 62 | 63 | 64 | 65 | 66 | 67 | 68 | 69 | 70 |

75

Up to eighty

Add the missing numbers to the snake to count to 80.

80
eighty

1 2 3 4 5 6 7

17 16 15 14 13 12 11 10 9 8

18 19 20 21 22 23 25 26 27 28

37 36 35 34 33 32 31 30 29

39 40 41 42 44 45 46 47 48

58 57 55 54 53 52 51 50 49

59

60 61 63 64 65 66 67 68

79 78 76 69

80 75 74 73 72 71 70

71 72 73 74 75 76 77 78 79 80

Up to ninety

Find the missing bugs and count to 90.

ninety

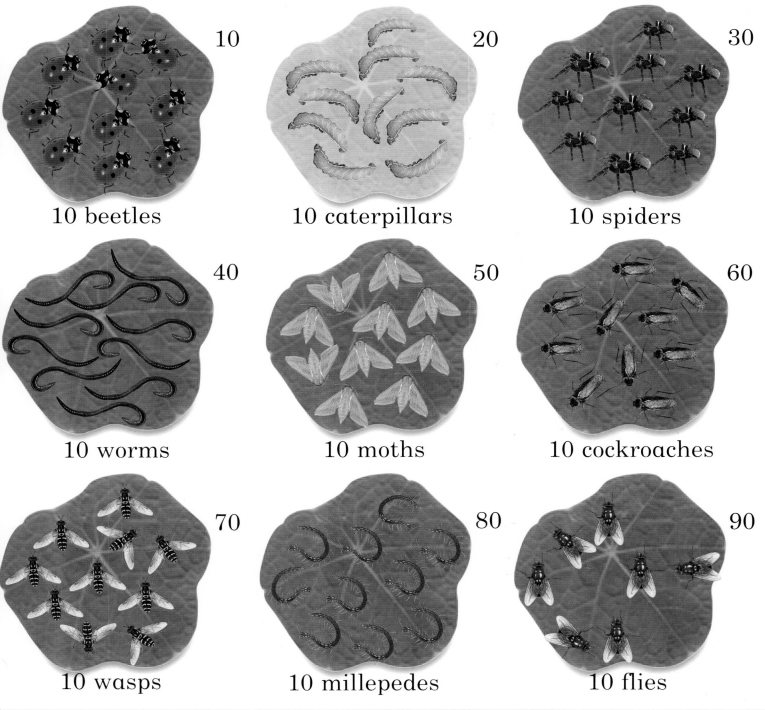

10   10 beetles

20   10 caterpillars

30   10 spiders

40   10 worms

50   10 moths

60   10 cockroaches

70   10 wasps

80   10 millepedes

90   10 flies

81   82   83   84   85   86   87   88   89   90

Up to one hundred

There are 100 things to
eat altogether.

one hundred

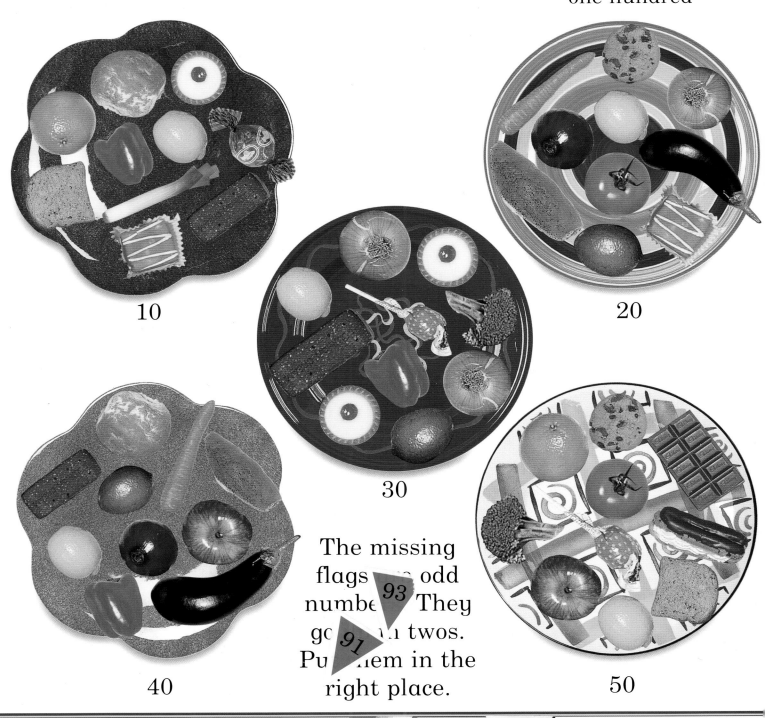

10

20

30

40

50

The missing
flags are odd
numbers. They
go up in twos.
Put them in the
right place.

93

91

92

94

95

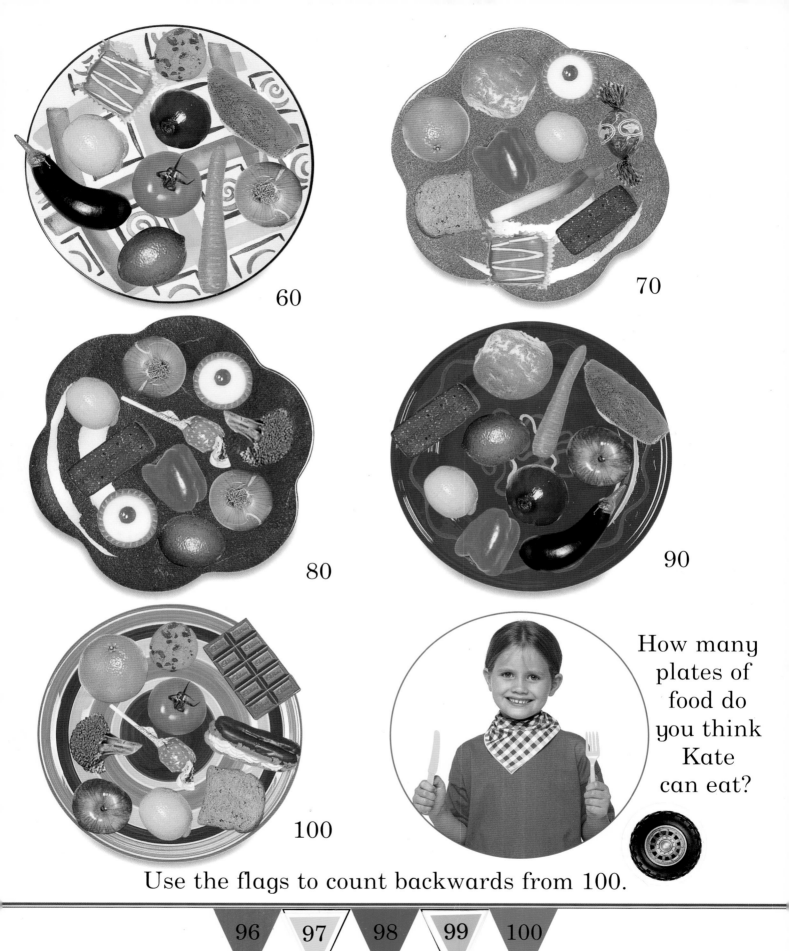

60

70

80

90

100

How many plates of food do you think Kate can eat?

Use the flags to count backwards from 100.

96 97 98 99 100

Snakes and ladders

Find some friends to play a game of snakes and ladders.

You will need:

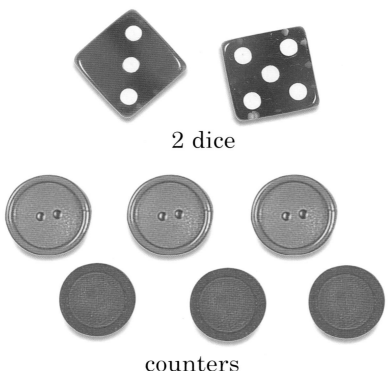

2 dice

counters

Stick the stickers on to the board. Choose a counter. Start at square number 1. Throw the dice and count the spots, this is your score. Your score will tell you how many squares to move along the board. If you land on the bottom of a ladder, climb up to the top. If you land on the head of a snake, then slide down to the end of the snake. The first one to get to 100 wins!

80

FINISH 100	99	98
81	82	83
80	79	78
61	62	63
60	59	58
41	42	43
40	39	38
21	22	23
20	19	18
START 1	2	3

97	96	95	94	93	92	91
84	85	86	87	88	89	90
77	76	75	74	73	72	71
64	65	66	67	68	69	70
57	56	55	54	53	52	51
44	45	46	47	48	49	50
37	36	35	34	33	32	31
24	25	26	27	28	29	30
17	16	15	14	13	12	11
4	5	6	7	8	9	10

Adding together

+

This means plus
or added to.

=

This means equals
or how many there are.

Two surprise
presents...

added to a pile
of seven presents.

How many surprise
presents are there now?

 + **7** **=** **9**

Three crabs balance
on each other...

plus another crab
for you to find.

equals four
balancing crabs.

3 **+** **1** **=** **4**

  0 **1** **2** **3** **4** **5** **6** **7** **8** **9** **10**

Doubling up

  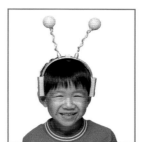

One lonely alien

Can you find him an alien friend?

Two friendly aliens

1 + 1 = 2

Two insects swing on the trapeze.

Two more insects swing towards them.

Four insects swing altogether now.

2 + 2 = 4

Three cuddly kittens are playing.

Three more cuddly kittens join in the fun.

Now six cuddly kittens play together.

3 + 3 = 6

More and more

One happy
puppy playing.

He has no friends
to play with.

So how many happy
puppies are there?

1 **+** **0** **=**

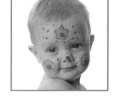

Two faces painted
for a party.

Find one more
painted face.

Makes
a party
of three!

2 **+** **1** **=** **3**

Three sleek
horses

Four more sleek
horses join them.

How many horses
altogether?

3 **+** **4** **=**

Have fun with sums!

Two teddy bears zoom along on their scooter.	Three teddy bears collide with them!	Oh, no! Five bears in a heap!

2 + 3 = 5

Jenny has counted six fingers.	Now she's counted three fingers.	How many has she counted altogether?

6 + 3 = ☐

One cold drink is no good if you are very thirsty.	Two more drinks will help – can you find them?	But three cold drinks will quench your thirst.

1 + 2 = 3

How fast can you add these?

Three ringing telephones

Two more suddenly start to ring.

Five telephones ringing makes such a noise!

3 + 2 = 5

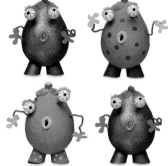  

Find the four potato heads.

Here are four more potato heads.

How many are there now?

4 + 4 = ☐

Eight dragon brothers and sisters

Can you find their two dragon cousins?

All ten make a big dragon family.

8 + 2 = 10

Fruity feast

Count the four types of fruit marked on the page. Stick the answers in the boxes.

How many strawberries can you count? Stick your answer here.

How many oranges can you count? Stick your answer here.

How many pineapples can you count? Stick your answer here.

How many bunches of grapes can you count? Stick your answer here.

Now add your answers together and stick the total here.

10 + 7 + 2 + 4 =

in a fruit salad

It's time to take away

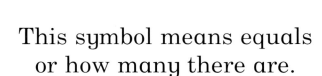

This symbol means minus or take away.

This symbol means equals or how many there are.

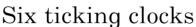

Six ticking clocks

Take two away.

How many clocks are left?

6 **–** **2** **=**

Can you find the third footprint?

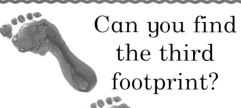

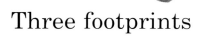

Three footprints

Two footprints are walking away.

Equals one footprint

3 **–** **2** **=** **1**

88 0   1   2   3   4   5   6   7   8   9   10

Fewer and fewer

Eight ripe bananas

The naughty monkey steals four of them.

How many bananas are left over?

8 **−** **4** **=** ☐

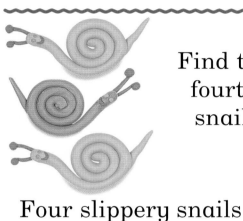

Find the fourth snail.

Four slippery snails

One snail slips away.

How many slippery snails are left?

4 **−** **1** **=** ☐

The baby bear has five shiny balloons.

But three fly away!

Stick how many balloons the bear has left here.

5 **−** **3** **=** **2**

There are even fewer here

Seven pieces of
cheese on
the board

The hungry mouse
nibbles away five of them.

Can you find the
two pieces of
cheese left over?

7 − 5 = 2

③

The wombat
balances
three pine
cones on
his head.

Then two fall
off!

Stick any
cones that
are left on
his head.

3 − 2 = 1

Three drumming
teddy bears

One marches
away on his own.

How many teddy
bears are left?

3 − 1 =

More of minus

Six treasure chests

The pirate teddy bear steals one.

How many treasure chests are left?

6 − **1** = [ ]

Nine space teddy bears

Seven are left floating. How many flew away?

9 − [ ] = **7**

Seven jack-in-the-boxes

Find the jack-in-the-box that was put in the cupboard.

There are just six left.

7 − **1** = **6**

91

Tumbling numbers

Ten buckets of sand

The sunbathing teddy bear carries away two.

How many buckets of sand are left?

10 **–** **2** **=** ☐

Eight bales of hay

The tractor scoops up one of them.

How many bales of hay are left?

8 **–** **1** **=** ☐

The frog balances four cupcakes on his feet.

Can you find the two cupcakes that fell off?

Two are left balancing.

4 **–** **2** **=** **2**

More taking away

Ten yummy chocolates

But no chocolates have been eaten!

Find all the chocolates that are left.

10 – 0 = 10

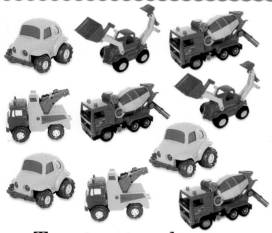

Ten toy trucks

Find one truck driving away.

How many trucks are left?

10 – 1 = ☐

One happy peanut

Elephant eats it!

How many peanuts are left?

1 – 1 = ☐

93

Mixed up sum fun

Count the number of shoes on the page and stick the answer in the first box.

Count the number of teddy bears on the page and stick the answer in the second box.

Now do the sum.

Stick the answer here.

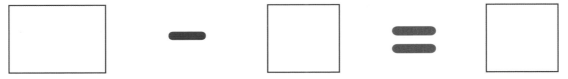

94

Create your own sums!

Add the four sticker symbols to these
four sums to make the answers right.

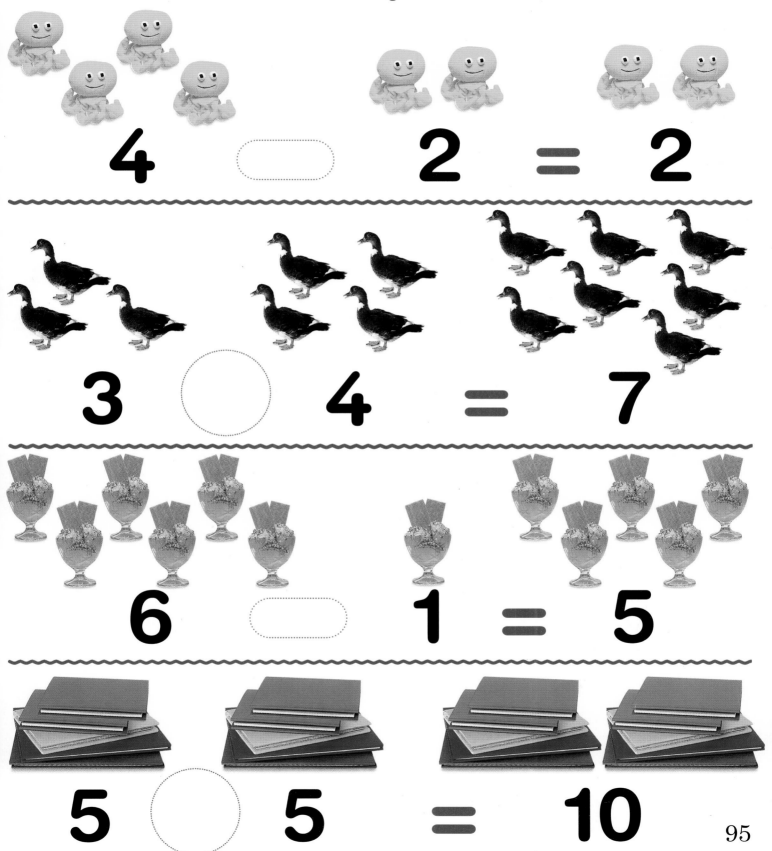

4 ⬭ 2 = 2

3 ◯ 4 = 7

6 ⬭ 1 = 5

5 ◯ 5 = 10

95

Time

What time do you get up?

Find the clock that says 6 o'clock

How fast can you eat cake?

What time do you eat lunch?

How many seconds are
in a minute?

What time of day do you
like best?

What time do you go to bed?

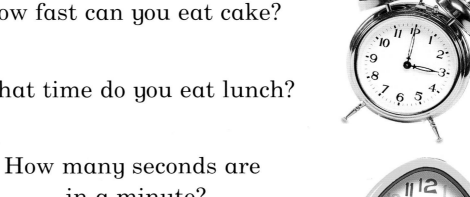

Time of day

Our days are divided into different parts.

I'm off to playgroup.

morning

It's time to wake up.

breakfast

Find someone else eating lunch.

afternoon

lunch

playtime

evening

storytime

supper

Shhh! It's bedtime.

Taking time

Everything you do takes time.

Some things take a short time.

Some things can take a long time.

Is it faster to bake a cake...

... or to eat one?

Find something that takes a long time.

Who will finish first?

Find something that takes a short time.

99

Telling the time

We use watches and clocks to tell the time.

alarm clock

yellow clock

clown clock

Find another wristwatch.

digital clock

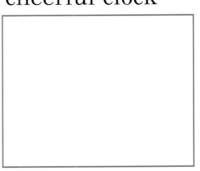

A stopwatch can time a race.

cheerful clock

cuckoo clock

Can you find another clock?

Our day

Take a look at the different things we do during the day.

7 o'clock

It's Jonathon's breakfast time.

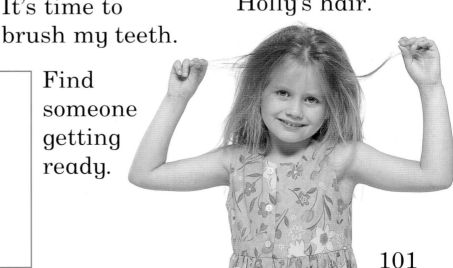

At 7am Rebecca wakes up.

Find some puppies eating breakfast.

I dress myself!

It's time to brush my teeth.

8 o'clock

Time to brush Holly's hair.

Find someone getting ready.

101

9 o'clock

playtime

Find two more clocks that say 9 o'clock.

Daisy goes to playgroup.

Time to g to the zoo

10 o'clock

Rosie washes the car. Add more buckets.

Time to build.

Find another busy builder.

Hope I finish painting by lunchtime!

11 o'clock

Time for a walk.

How many can I do?

stretching time

Lifting at eleven.

Find two more teddy bears exercising at 11am.

12 o'clock

Time for some crisp lettuce.

Find some yummy fruit for lunch.

Oops, I'm late for lunch.

It's always pizza time!

Lunchtime for Jonathon.

103

1 o'clock

quiet time

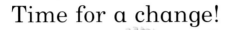

Find another sleepy puppy.

You need an afternoon nap.

Time for a change!

It's storytime for teddy bear.

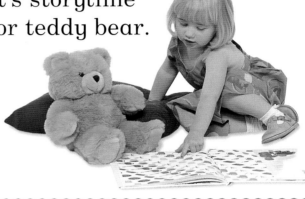

2 o'clock

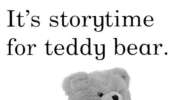

Shake, rattle, swing and sing time!

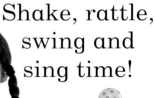

How long will this take me to do?

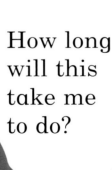

What is Tom doing at 2pm?

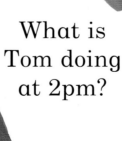

Find the rest of the 2 o'clock band.

It's outdoor playtime!

3 o'clock

Find some tasty snacks to share at 3 o'clock.

What else can you play with outside?

water play

I'm hungry!

4 o'clock

flower arranging at four

Time to clean up!

Have you got time to make a neat stack?

I've been shopping!

105

5 o'clock

It's supper time!

Time for a treat!

What are these children having for supper today?

6 o'clock

Can you find some bathtime whales?

I'll read you a bedtime story.

I brush my teeth before bed.

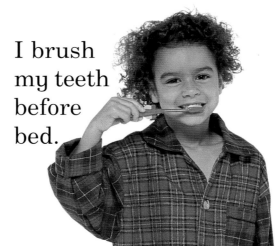

Find a bathtime baby.

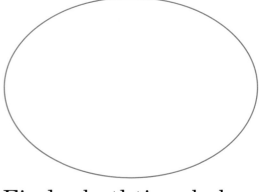

Half hours

The big hand takes half an hour to move halfway around the clock face.

Two halves make a whole.

2 o'clock

It's half past two.

Where's the other half?

Find a clock showing half past.

Quarters

A quarter of an hour is fifteen minutes.

How many quarters make a whole?

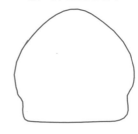

Find a clock showing quarter past six.

quarter past two

It's a quarter to two.

What time is it?   107

Wait a minute!

How many minutes does it take you to...

The big hand is called the minute hand.

...tie your shoelaces?

...build a tower?

...hop across the room?

...catch a fish?

If you count to five slowly, that's about five seconds.

Can you balance for one minute?

On time

We have to do some things at a certain time.

What time's take-off?

Teddy Bear missed his plane.

It's time for the 5 o'clock special!

Find a clock showing 5pm.

We'll be late if we stop. Find some more ants.

109

Around the clock

Can you find the right clocks
to go with the activities?

It's half past
seven already!

I do my morning
exercises at 8 o'clock.

It's
10 o'clock
and I'm nearly
finished!

Breakfast at 8am.

Time for
lunch at
12 o'clock.

Washing
at
9 o'clock.

It's 1 o'clock, our nap time.

At 2 o'clock, it's playtime.

In the park at 3 o'clock.

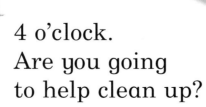

4 o'clock. Are you going to help clean up?

Getting ready for bed at 5 o'clock.

Sleepyheads at 7 o'clock.

Time to go!

111

Simple Science

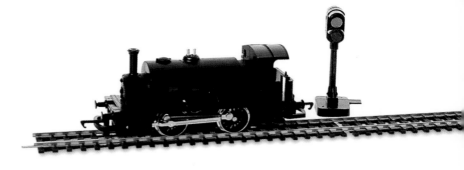

A green light means go.

Look out, there's
a car coming.

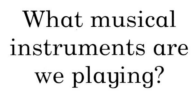

Pulling a heavy
bag is hard work.

Spinning tops go
round and round.

What musical
instruments are
we playing?

I can move quickly
on my scooter.

Movement

Things can move quickly or slowly and in different directions.

Spinning tops go round and round.

A red light means stop!

Harriet is moving slowly.

Lisa is moving quickly.

A green light means the train can go ahead.

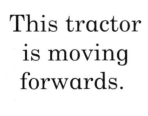

This tractor is moving forwards.

Choose the sticker toys who want to ride in the trucks.

Push and pull

You can move things when you push and pull them.

Pushing a swing makes it move.

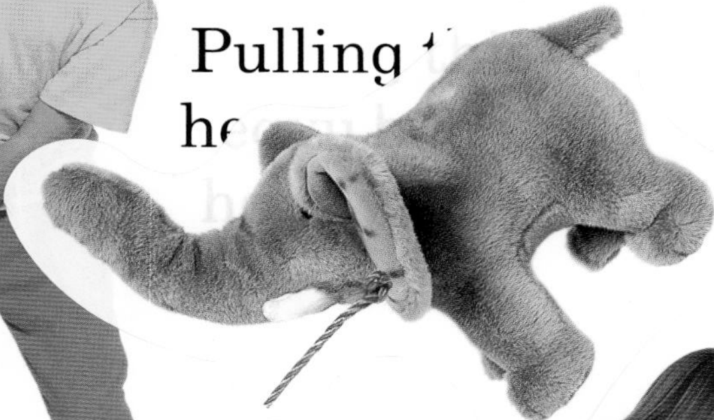

Pulling the

Pushing the go-cart makes it go.

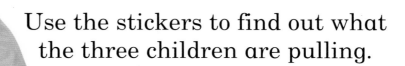

Use the stickers to find out what the three children are pulling.

115

Float and sink

Some things are light and float on water. Others are heavy and sink.

Help the bear find out what floats and what sinks.

A balloon floats.

Find some more light things that float.

A ball an float

A swimmer floats in the sea.

Find some heavy things that sink

sunken treasure chest

Pebbles sink to the bottom.

are to float.

Air and wind

You can't see it but it is all around you. Wind is air that moves from place to place.

When you breathe in, air goes into your lungs.

Wind makes kites fly.

Can you blow bubbles full of air?

Find some more bubbles.

My hair is blowing around in the wind!

Find some more wind-blown leaves.

117

Temperature

Hot and cold things feel different to touch.

Hot water bottles make your feet warm.

Your cooker cools es in the warm sun.

Find some clothes to keep you warm.

Hot drinks warm you up in winter.

A hot oven turns this mixture into a delicious cake.

Fans make
air move
to cool
you down.

Snow is
water that
is so cold,
it freezes.

Find some cold food
and drink to stick here.

Freezing water
makes ice.

Cold
drinks
cool you
down.

119

Bodies

Every body has lots of different parts.
Some you can see, but others are hidden.

This is what I look like inside!

head

arm

hip

hand

leg

knee

foot

Find my missing body parts.

You can feel blood pumping through your wrist.

This is what your heart looks like.

Balance

If something is balanced, it will not fall over.

Now she is balanced on her skates.

Oh, no! Emma has lost her balance and fallen down.

Is this seesaw balanced?

Is it now?

Find Freddy Frog's pals to balance on the tightrope.

Touch and feel

We feel with our skin.
When we touch, it tells us
what something is like.

Ouch!

My sweater
feels scratchy!

I've
touched
a prickly
holly bush.

My sweater
feels soft
and warm.

A kiwi
fruit is
hairy to
touch.

Stick things
that are soft to
touch here.

Stick things
that are prickly
to touch here.

Nature

Animals, plants and insects are all part of Nature.

flower

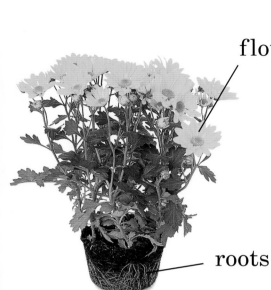

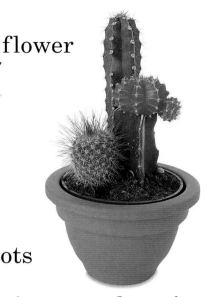

roots

These flowers have roots.

A cactus doesn't need much water.

Flowers need water to grow.

Rabbits have soft furry coats.

Find some insects that collect nectar from flowers.

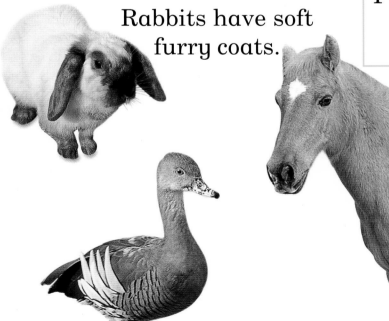

Ducks have feathers.

Horses have short hairy coats.

123

Hearing sounds

Sounds are made by moving air. Our ears hear sounds.

What can you hear?

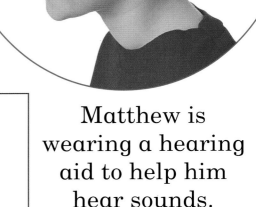

Matthew is wearing a hearing aid to help him hear sounds.

Find some things that make different noises.

Is anybody there?

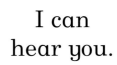

I can hear you.

Musical instruments make special sounds.

strumming guitar

Kate sings along with her band.

loud drum

scraping scratcher

tinkly xylophone

clashing cymbals

Find some more musical instruments for the band.

All kinds of science

You can have fun looking at science all around you.

Who will move quicker, Daisy or Tim?

Find more stepping stones for Sophie to step on.

Balance the cookies on the plate.

Hold some chocolate in your hand. Will it get warm or cold?

Look in your home for some hard and soft things.

soft flower

Find some more hard apples.

soft strawberries

What type of coat does a dog have?

How long will this take to melt?

Touch some ice and see how it feels.

Can you touch your nose and your ear?

Th... ...blished in 2002 by Hermes House

...Publishing Limited 2002

Herm... ...imprint of Anness Publishing Limited
Herme... ...-89 Blackfriars R... London SE1 8HA

Published in the USA ...es House
Anness Pub...
27 West 20th Street, ... 10...

A CIP cata... ...ord for this book is available
from the British Library.

Publisher: Joanna Lorenz
Managing Editor, Children's Books:
Gilly Cameron Cooper
Editors: Jennifer Davidson, Rasha Elsaeed,
Sarah Uttridge
Authors: Jayne Miller, Jenni Rainford, Jennifer Davidson
Educational Consultant: Joanna Babb
Editorial Reader: Joy Wotton
Design and Typesetting: Michael and James Leaman,
Roger McWilliam, Ann Samuel, Rachael Stone,
Sarah Williams, Alix Wood
Jacket Design: Alix Wood of Applecart
Production Controller: Steve Lang

The publishers wish to th... ...ll the child...
o...

Previously p... ...s ...ite
in ...er ...s:
*Action, Count ... y Body, Making Groups,
Simple Science ... Sums, Time* and *Words.*

1 3 5 7 9 10 8 6 4 2

Stickers page 6

page 7

page 8

page 9

page 10

bookcase   rug

table   bin

cushion

cups

mug

chair

soaps   toothpaste   bubble bath   hairbrush

page 11

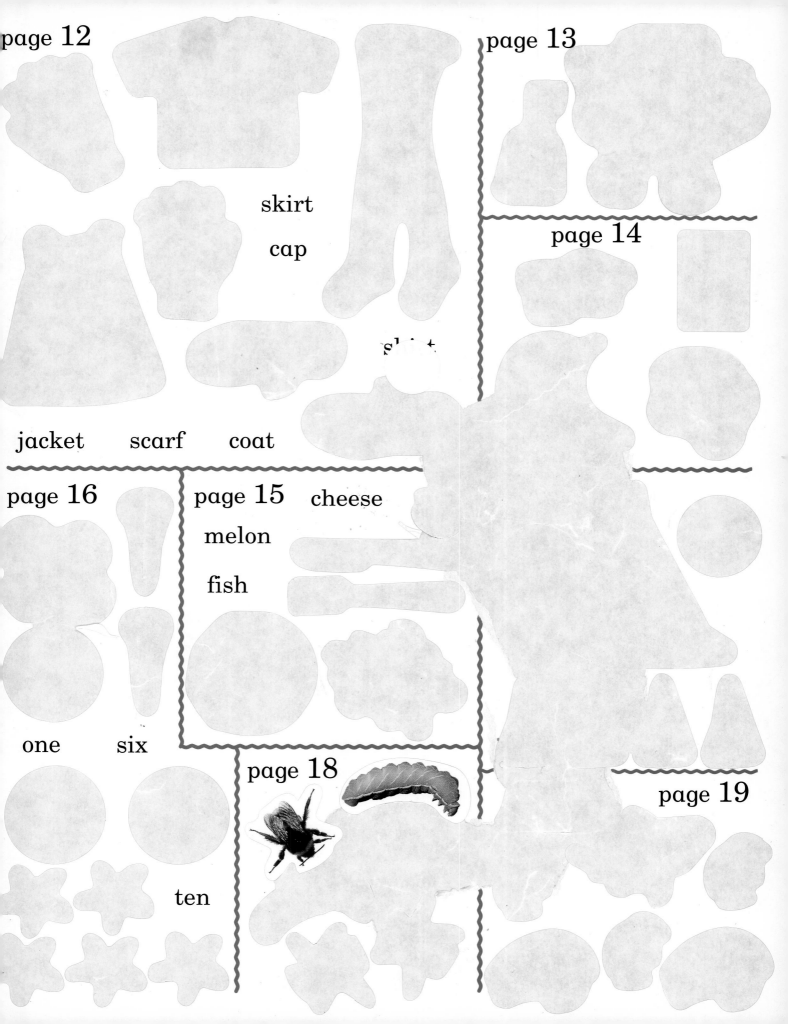

page 12

page 13

skirt

cap

page 14

shirt

jacket   scarf   coat

page 16

page 15   cheese

melon

fish

one   six

page 18

page 19

ten

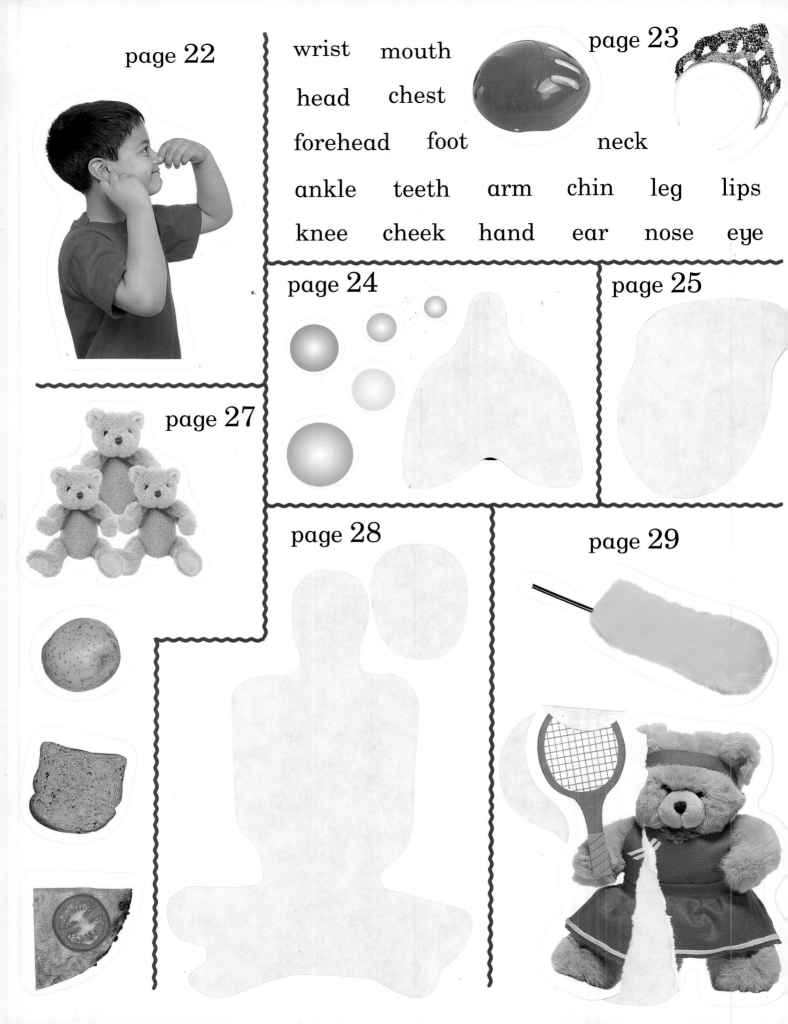

page 22

page 23

wrist   mouth
head   chest
forehead   foot   neck
ankle   teeth   arm   chin   leg   lips
knee   cheek   hand   ear   nose   eye

page 24

page 25

page 27

page 28

page 29

page 30

page 31

ge 32

page 3.

page 34

35

taller

shorte.

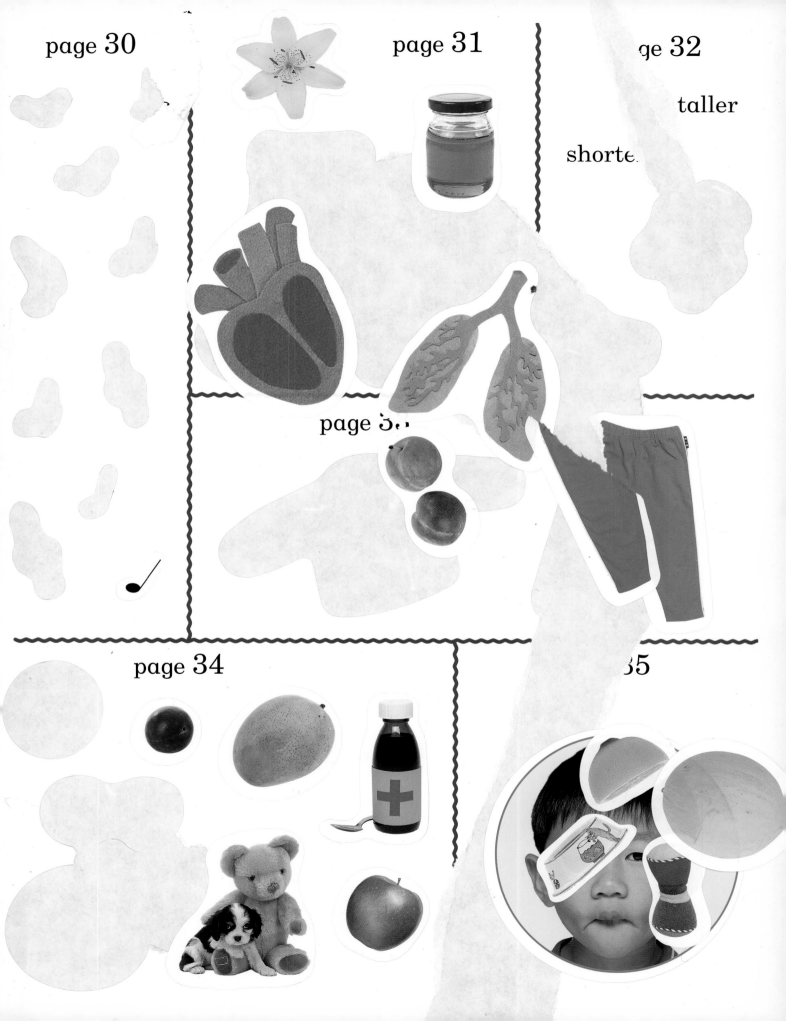

page 36

page 37

page 38

page 39

page 40

page 41

page 42

page 43

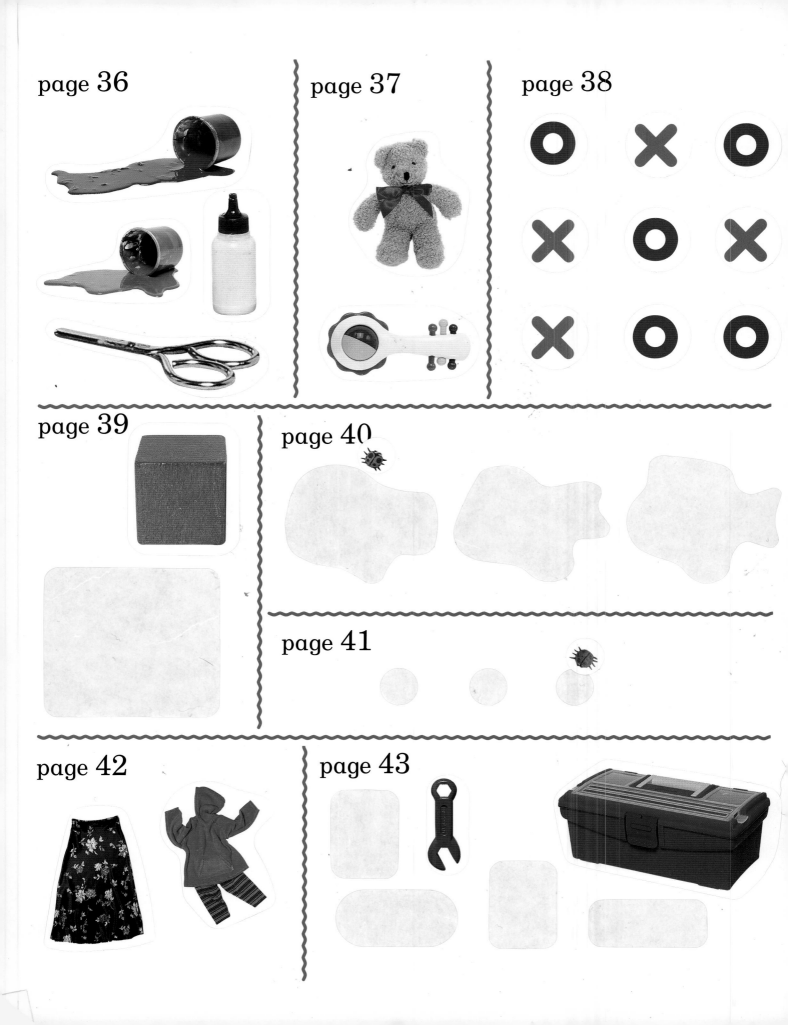

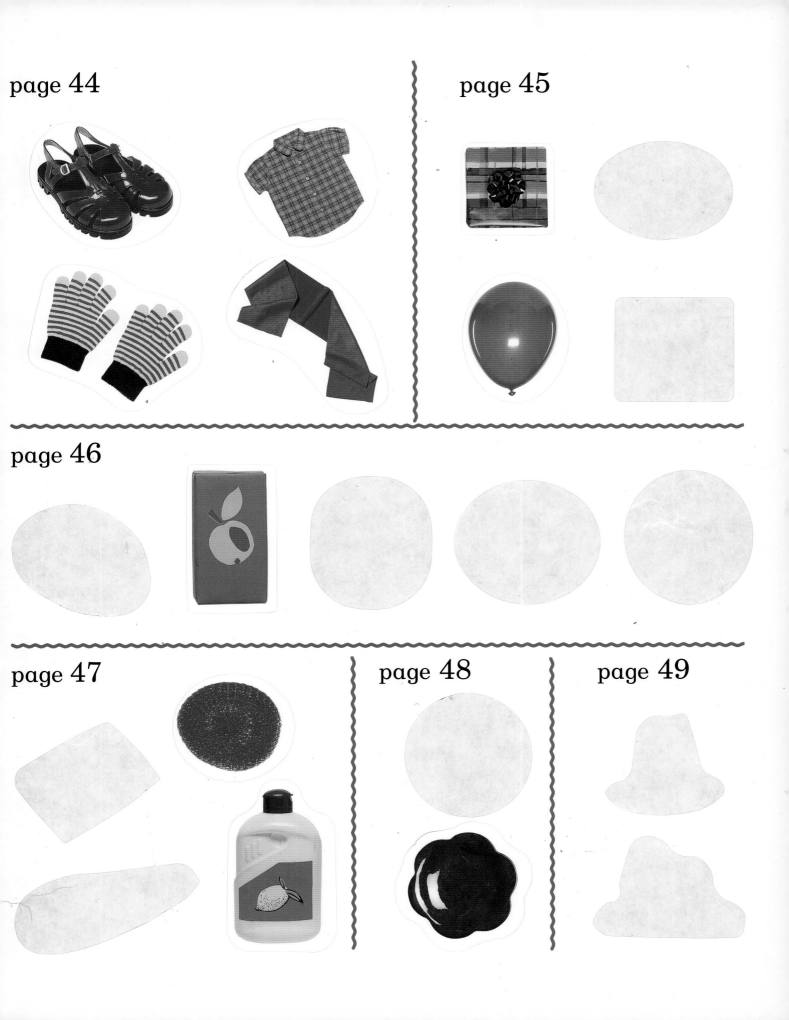

page 44

page 45

page 46

page 47

page 48

page 49

page 52

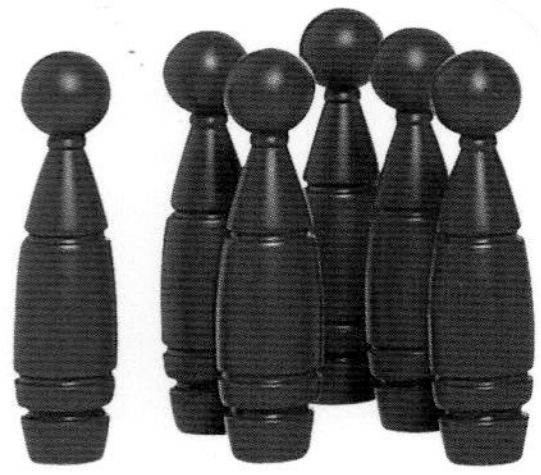

page 53

page 54

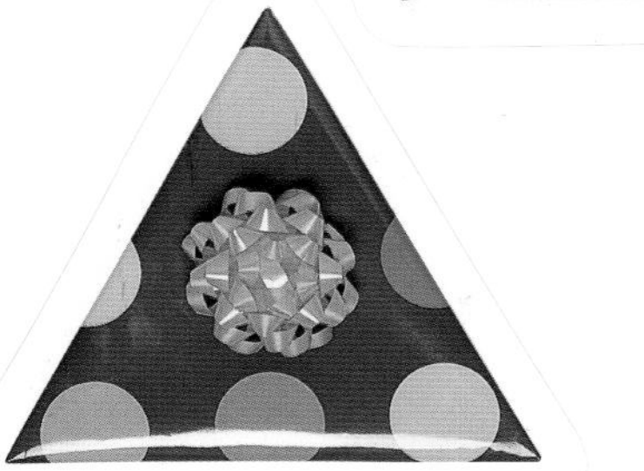

page 55

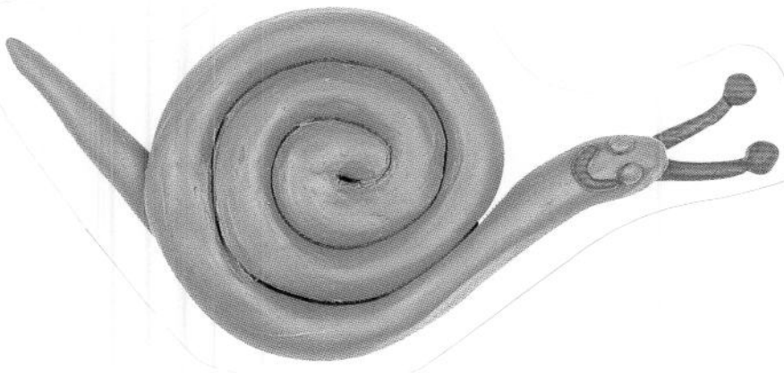

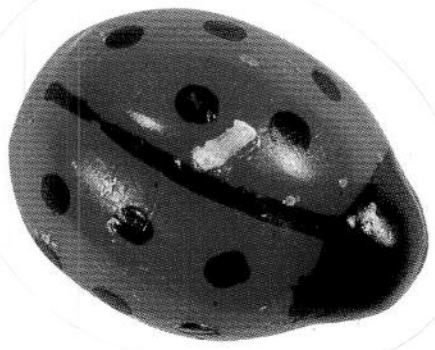

page 56

page 57

page 58

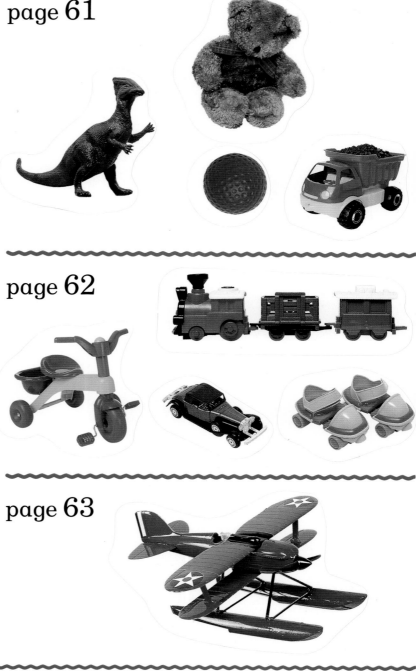

page 59

bottom part

sport

night clothes

top part

page 60

page 61

page 62

page 63

page 64

blue

square

spots

summer

page 65

bedtime

cuddly toys

fruit

in the air

page 68

page 69

1
2
3
4
5
7
6
8
10
9

page 70

43
62

77
56
38
24

13

16

19

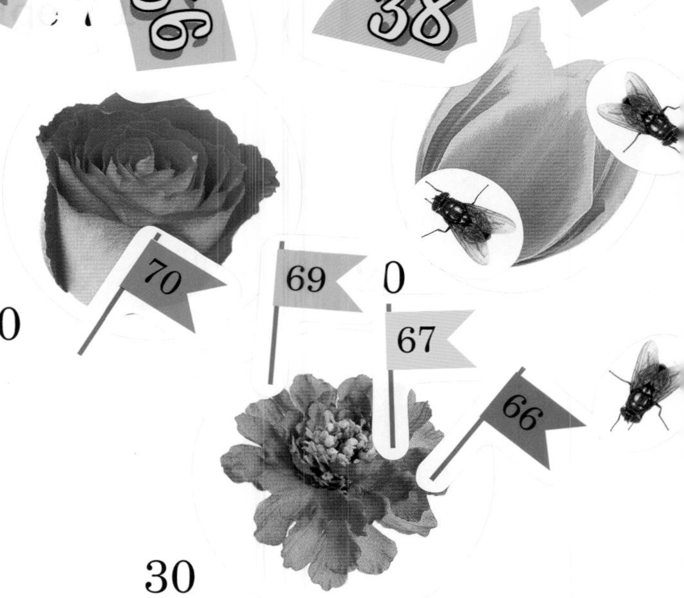

10

70
69
0
67
66

30

page 72

20

25

40

page 73

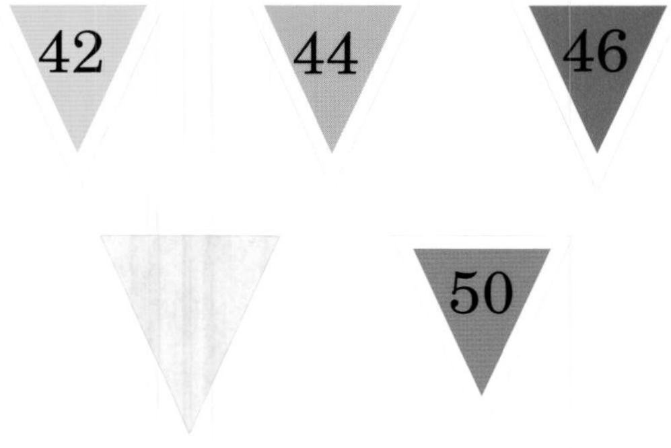

42
44
46

50

page 74

20 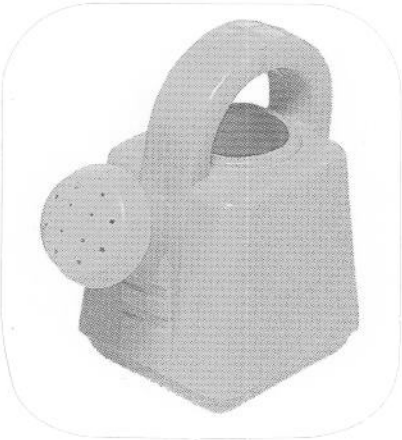   30    50 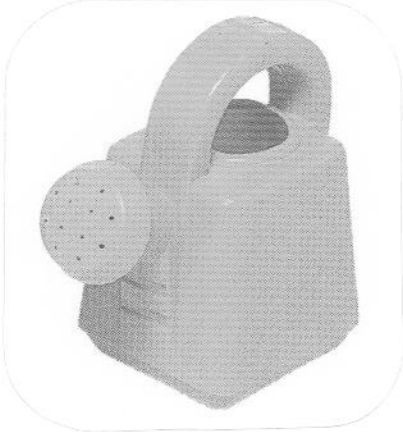   60

page 75

63 64 65 62

page 76

page 77

pages 78 and 79

pages 80 and 81

page 82

page 83

page 84

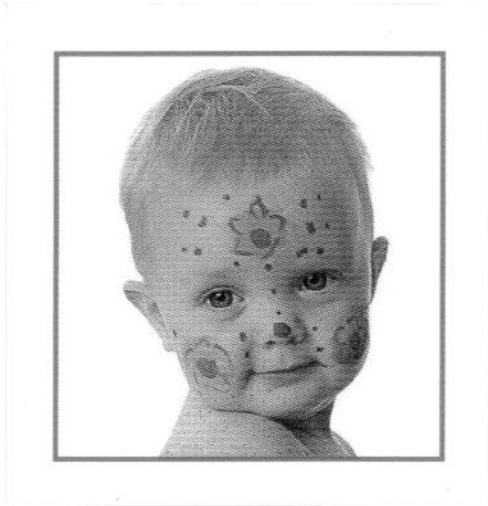

1

7

page 85

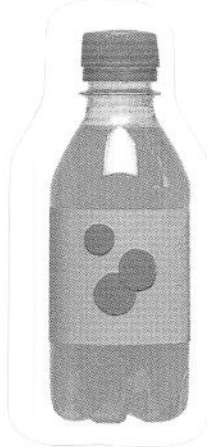

9

page 86

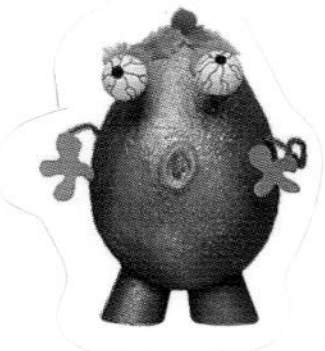

8

page 88

page 87

2 **4** **7** **10** **23**

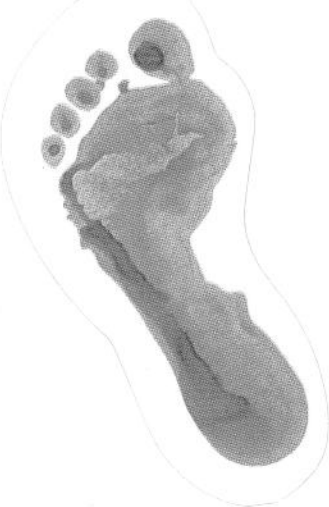

4

page 89

3   **4**

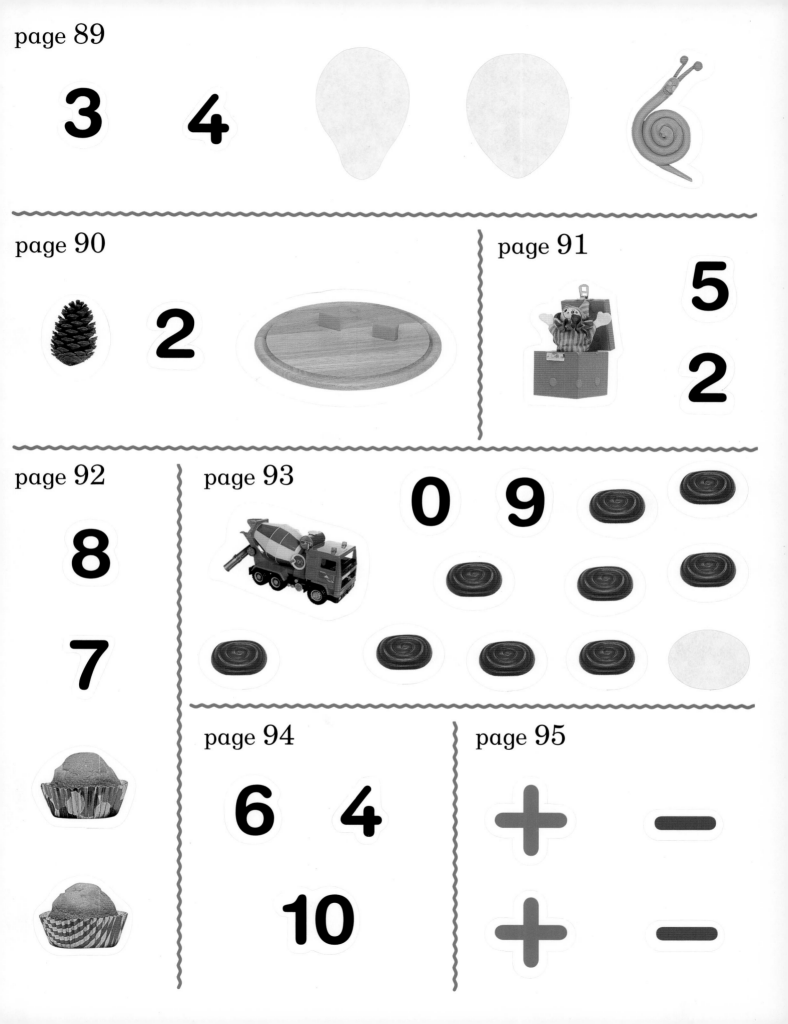

page 90

2

page 91

5

2

page 92

8

7

page 93

0   **9**

page 94

6   **4**

10

page 95

+   **−**

+   **−**

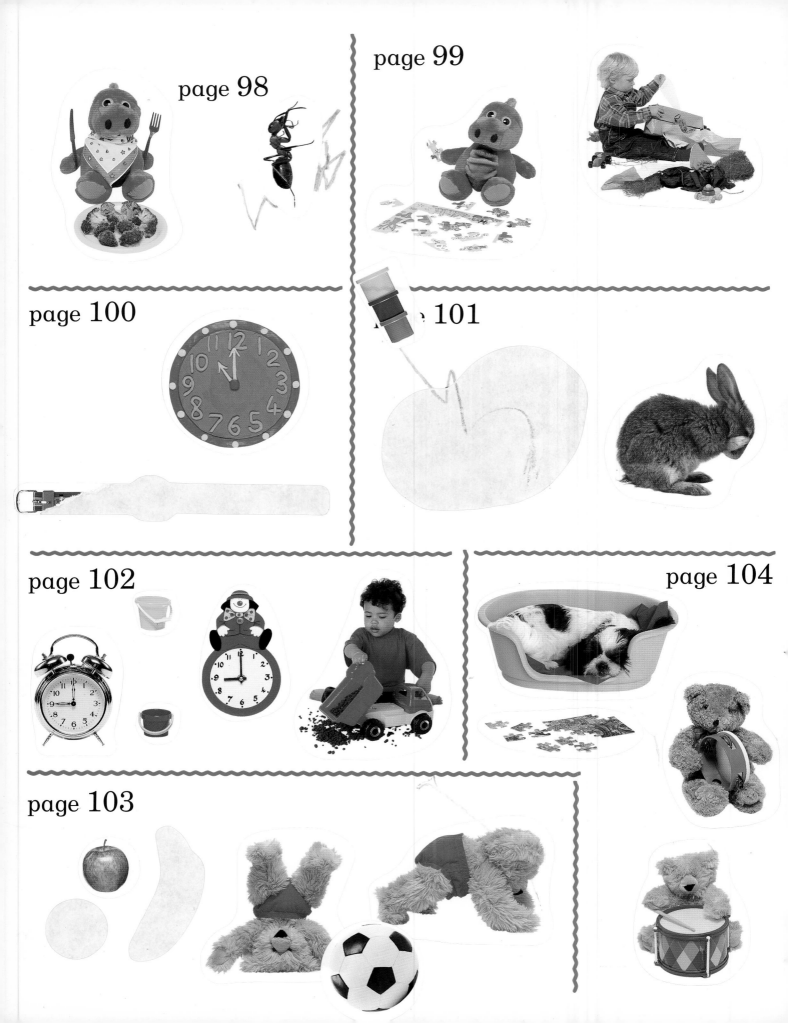

page 98

page 99

page 100

page 101

page 102

page 104

page 103

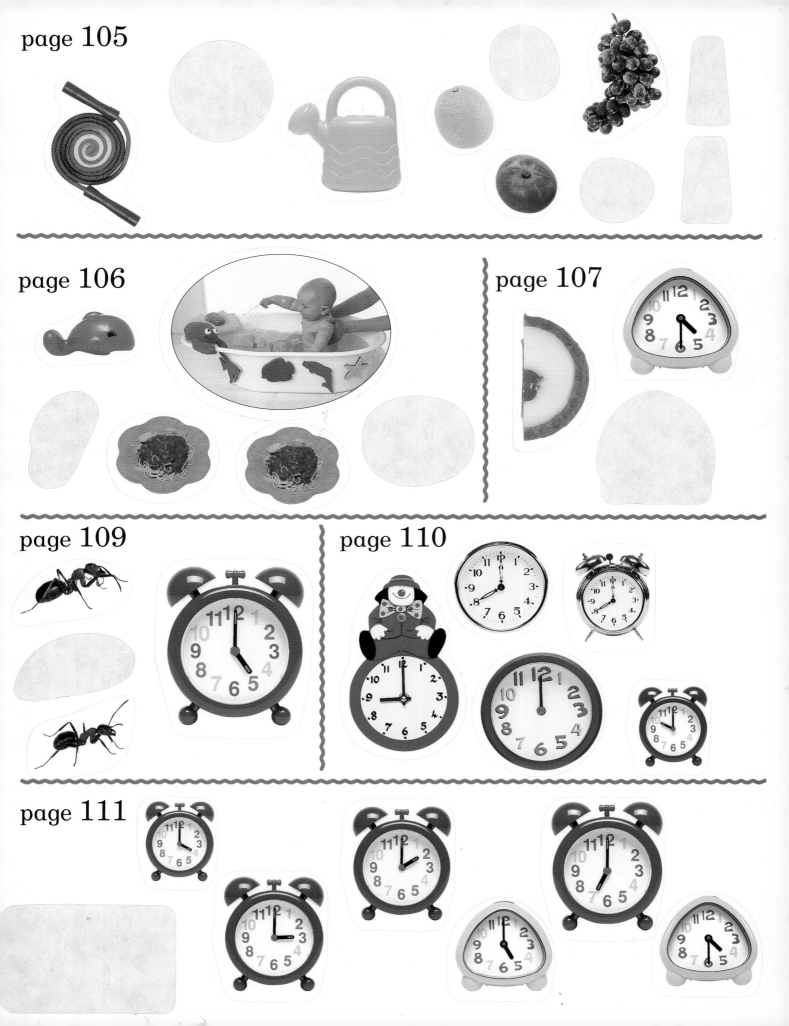

page 105

page 106

page 107

page 109

page 110

page 111

page 120 | arm | leg |
| hand | foot |

page 121

page 122

page 124

page 123

page 125

page 1

page 127

page 114

page 115

page 116

page 117

pages 118 and 119

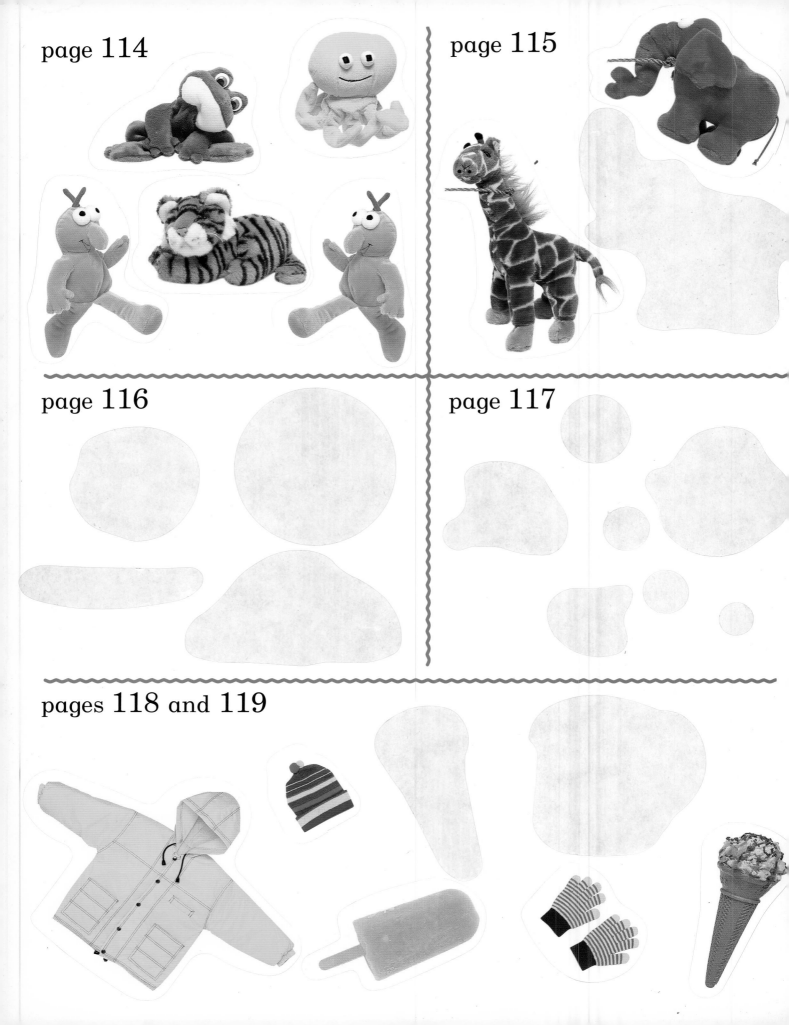